Praise for *Stories That Stick*

"Whatever you do, wherever you are in your career, this is the book to read right now. Practical, funny and true, Kindra's new book is a keeper."

> —SETH GODIN, *NEW YORK TIMES* BESTSELLING
> AUTHOR OF *THIS IS MARKETING*

"Storytelling is an essential business skill. It makes data more compelling and communication more effective. In her book, Kindra Hall makes storytelling accessible to anyone. You don't have to be a great writer to tell great stories—you just need to know how to tell *Stories That Stick*."

> —CHARLES DUHIGG, BESTSELLING AUTHOR OF *THE*
> *POWER OF HABIT* AND *SMARTER FASTER BETTER*

"Here's the story: your business is in its current state, you buy this book, read it in one sitting like I did, have your mind blown, your business greatly improves. End scene. Lots of people tell stories, a few are great at it and one can show you how to do it. That's the story of Kindra and this book."

> —SCOTT STRATTEN, BESTSELLING, AWARD-WINNING AUTHOR
> AND HALL OF FAME SPEAKER/STORYTELLER

"I'm picky about what I read. Doubly so with business books. But Kindra hooked me on page one and wouldn't let go. Such is the power of superb storytelling. If you want to inspire your customers and your team, craft a vision that resonates, and do better marketing, *Stories That Stick* is essential reading."

> —RAND FISHKIN, FOUNDER OF SPARKTORO

"Storytelling is an art form often lost today among snippets, sound bites, and buzzword copy. Which is unfortunate, because story is how we've connected with each other since language began. In *Stories That Stick*, Kindra Hall beautifully weaves the argument for story with the best way to craft one. Advice every business owner and influencer needs to understand."

> —MEL ROBBINS, AUTHOR OF THE INTERNATIONAL
> BESTSELLER *THE 5 SECOND RULE*

"Timely, personal, poignant, and powerful, *Stories That Stick* is required reading to grow your business with the power of stories. Highly recommended!"
    —Jay Baer, founder of Convince & Convert,
        coauthor of *Talk Triggers*

"In my business, telling a personal story is the essence to authenticity, and proof that what I do and who I help really achieves results. Stories share a journey that me and my team can identify with and provide a way to personally connect with our clients."
    —Autumn Calabrese, Entrepreneur,
        fitness and nutrition expert

Stories
THAT
Stick

Stories
THAT
Stick

How Storytelling Can
Captivate Customers, Influence Audiences,
and Transform Your Business

KINDRA HALL

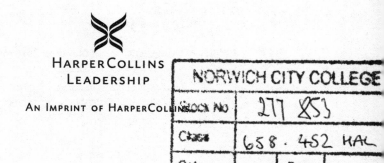

HARPERCOLLINS
LEADERSHIP

AN IMPRINT OF HARPERCOLLINS

Published by HarperCollins Leadership, an imprint of HarperCollins Focus LLC.

Any internet addresses, phone numbers, or company or product information printed in this book are offered as a resource and are not intended in any way to be or to imply an endorsement by HarperCollins Leadership, nor does HarperCollins Leadership vouch for the existence, content, or services of these sites, phone numbers, companies, or products beyond the life of this book.

ISBN 978-1-4002-1194-4 (eBook)
ISBN 978-1-4002-1193-7 (HC)

Library of Congress Control Number: 2018967126

Printed in the United States of America
21 22 23   LSC   10 9 8

To the one who wonders if you have a story to tell, if you can tell it, or if you should tell it, this book is for you. And the answer is yes, three times.

Contents

Introduction

Slovenia, JFK, and the Story That Kidnapped My Husband

It was Thanksgiving weekend. Six thousand miles away, people were eating turkey and mashed potatoes, sharing what they were grateful for, and passing out on couches with the dull roar of football playing in the background.

I was doing none of those things . . . because I was in Slovenia.

I'll be honest. "I'm in Slovenia" is not something I ever imagined I would say—except for that one time I met a Slovenian soccer player while on vacation in Mexico and was convinced for a day that I would marry him. And yet there I was. There *we* were. My husband, Michael (who does not play soccer), and I were wandering around the quaint, slightly damp cobblestone streets of Ljubljana, Slovenia's capital. And though we missed Thanksgiving, I felt distinctly grateful. Not only for the fairy tale city we had just stepped into . . .

But because I'd just heard one of the best sales stories of my life.

Before I go any further, I should tell you something. Stories are my life. They are my work, my currency, the way I see the world. I told my first story when I was eleven years old. And ever since that day, stories have followed me, sought me, and now I spend my days speaking about using stories strategically and teaching others to tell theirs.

In fact, stories are the reason I was in Slovenia. I was invited from the United States specifically to speak to nearly one thousand marketing and brand managers, media execs, and advertising creatives from across Eastern Europe on the power of storytelling in business.

So you can imagine the irony, or at the very least the intrigue, when I—the story expert—witnessed the greatest story coup of all time.

It happened in the evening hours of that late November weekend. Though Slovenians don't celebrate Thanksgiving, the city was festive and alive as they celebrated the beginning of the holiday season with an annual tree-lighting ceremony. Michael and I walked among thousands of Slovenians enjoying local wine, chestnuts roasting on the open fires of street vendors, and more wine. The night sky was dark, the air was wet and chilled, and the streets glowed with soft, warm light from the Christmas décor suspended between every building. The faint sound of carols echoed from the city center, and the shop windows lining the streets sparkled, calling to us, inviting us to come in and explore.

Well, that's not entirely true. The shop windows were calling to *me*, not *us*. Shop windows do not call to Michael, because Michael does not shop. He doesn't window-shop, online-shop, bargain-shop, or anything-shop. He purchases almost no things. The elastic waistband of his underwear disintegrates before Michael buys another pair. He, in fact, may not even have a wallet.

As our European trip progressed, this fundamental difference in our shopping preferences developed into a rather repetitive conversation:

Me: Oh! A local designer's boutique. Let's check it out!
Michael: [Acts as if he didn't hear me. Keeps walking.]
Me: Oh! A local rug maker's shop. Let's check it out!

Michael: [Doesn't hear me. Keeps walking.]

Me: Oh! Everything in that shop is made of cork. Let's check it out!

Michael: [Pulls out his cell phone, though it doesn't work. Keeps walking.]

Me: Oh! Fresh bread!

Michael: [Takes a deep breath of baked-bread air. Keeps walking.]

This didn't offend me for two reasons. One, I'm used to it. And two, we had only brought two carry-ons for this weeklong trip. Not even the softest piece of bread would squeeze into our luggage, so I didn't put up much of a fight.

Until that night. Until I saw . . . the shoes.

There, sitting proudly in one of the gloriously lit windows, was a pair of show-stopping shoes.

They were silver. And sparkly. *Glittery* even. And perhaps it was all the wine (and lack of bread), but in that moment, I couldn't resist any longer. Before he knew what was happening, I dragged an unsuspecting Michael into an upscale boutique on a Ljubljanan side street.

Inside, the store was an eclectic mix of products, from watches and jewelry to art and clothing. I made a beeline for the shoes and left Michael to fend for himself near the fragrances.

To my great dismay, up close the shoes were atrocious. Blinding. I immediately felt a deep sense of guilt for abandoning Michael at the first glimpse of glitter. I ran back toward the front of the store where Michael was trying to hide behind a rotating tower of perfume bottles. Just as I was about to grab him and head outside to the safety of the cobblestones, a very ambitious twentysomething Slovenian sales clerk appeared, as if from thin air, from behind the fragrance counter, just inches from where Michael was standing and called to him.

"Excuse me, sir. Were you looking for a scent?"

Oh, no, I thought. *Oh, this poor kid is so far off . . .*

Michael was most definitely not looking for a scent. Not only because looking for a scent would imply purchasing a scent—which we've already covered—but because Michael does not wear cologne. Ever. He's not a scent kind of guy. He was only near the scent counter because he needed someplace to stand-slash-hide.

Which is exactly what I tried to tell the salesman, but he didn't seem to care. Instead, he delicately removed a navy-and-white striped box from an upper shelf of the display.

"This is our bestseller," he stated, his fingers (unusually long, I noticed) gently framed the box. We braced ourselves to be spritzed against our will.

But the salesman didn't even open the box. Instead, he put the unopened package down on the glass countertop and, with the slight smile of a man who knows what he's doing, began.

Eight & Bob

"This . . . is Eight & Bob.[1]

"In 1937, a young, handsome, American college student was touring the French Riviera. At twenty years old, there was something special about him. All who met him could sense a rising star."

The young clerk paused to see if we were listening. We were.

"One day this young man was out and about the town when he encountered a Frenchman by the name of Albert Fouquet, a Parisian aristocrat and perfume connoisseur.

"Of course, the young man doesn't know this. All he knows is the man smells *incredible*. Being quite charming, the ambitious American convinces Fouquet, who never sold his scents, to share a small sample of the irresistible cologne."

I glanced at Michael. He had yet to blink.

"As you can imagine, when the young man returned to the States, others were entranced by the scent as well, and if he wasn't irresistible before, he certainly was now. The young man knew he was on to something, so he wrote to Fouquet, imploring that he send eight more samples 'and one for Bob.'"

Though he didn't say anything, Michael's face asked the question the clerk answered next.

"You see, Bob was the young man's brother. And the young man, well, you probably know him as John. Or simply J."

The clerk's voice trailed off before the end of the sentence, and Michael, as if he had just discovered One-Eyed Willy's pirate treasure, whispered, "FK."

"Yes." The clerk nodded. "The young man in question was none other than John F. Kennedy. And the sample was for his brother, Robert."

At this point, I was no longer a participant in the interaction (if I ever was) but rather a spectator. While I wanted to know how the Eight & Bob story ended, I was more interested in the story that was happening before my eyes.

"This is JFK's cologne?" Michael said with wonder.

"Indeed, it is." The clerk continued. "Of course, as you know, international relations weren't always easy between the United States and France. And though I am no history expert, I do know that shipping bottles of cologne became increasingly more difficult. So, in order to protect the final shipments from the Nazis, the last few bottles were hidden—"

The clerk paused and looked at Michael, whose mouth may or may not have been hanging open.

"In books." On that cue, the clerk opened the box he'd pulled from the shelf so long ago. In the box was a book. He opened the book. And there, nestled inside the pages that had been perfectly cut away to frame its contents, was a beautiful crystal bottle of cologne.

At that moment Michael said three words I've never heard him say before.

"I'll take it."

How a Story Changes Everything

At this point one thing has become clear to me: my husband has been kidnapped and replaced with an impostor. A cologne-buying alien. A cologne, to be clear, Michael hasn't even smelled.

Truly, though, I know better. There is nothing alien about what happened to Michael in that Slovenian shop. In fact, his response to the clerk's efforts was the most human thing that could have happened.

Because stronger than a man's desire to keep his wallet closed . . .

More charming than JFK himself . . .

Is the irresistible power of a story. A perfectly placed, impeccably delivered story can transport a person to a place beyond interested, straight past paying attention, and into a state of complete captivation. The "can't look away" kind. The "oh shoot, I just missed my exit" kind. In these moments of story we are, like my husband that evening, seized in a way that feels almost beyond our control.

There's a reason it feels that way. As we'll see, when it comes to a great story, we really can't help ourselves. From the moment the sales clerk in that boutique began to tell the Eight & Bob story, a shift happened in us: a shift in our understanding, a shift in our desires.

This is the shift so many of us seek. Far beyond buying a bottle of cologne, the shift a story can make has a profound impact on business. It turns customers into converts. It transforms employees into evangelists. Executives into leaders. It changes the nature and impact of marketing, and perhaps most importantly, it can change how we see ourselves.

How that shift happens and how you can create it by harnessing the power of storytelling are what this book is about.

———

As fate would have it, the only bottle of Eight & Bob in the boutique that night was the sample we saw on the shelf. We couldn't even buy it. In his excitement to tell us the story, the clerk neglected to see if he had any in stock. But our inability to bring a bottle home in no way diminished Michael's enthusiasm. In fact, it fueled it.

My typically even-keeled husband was suddenly charged. As we left the boutique and I began a search for our next spot to drink wine, Michael spoke and gestured with the fervor of an impassioned European. He marveled over the great packaging of the product, so perfectly aligned with the story. He imagined the rare scent being snuck past the Nazis, arriving, perhaps in secret, at the White House. Mysterious books containing hidden bottles of cologne someday sitting on the desk of the president of the United States.

"We should try to get the distribution rights for North America," he said. "This stuff is amazing. Everyone should know about it."

Keep in mind: never once did we talk about what the cologne actually smelled like. It didn't matter. By the time we returned to our hotel that evening, we'd decided to go back to the store the next day in case a shipment arrived before we had to catch our flight home.

When we arrived the next morning, the sales clerk from the previous evening was gone. In his place, a middle-aged woman explained they were still out of Eight & Bob.

I was curious. "Can you tell us anything about the cologne?"

"Let's see," she mused. "There are five different scents in the product line. Uh," she struggled, "they use unique plants from, um, France. It seems very popular. The packaging is nice." Then she ran out of steam. That was it.

The difference between the two experiences was shocking. As if yesterday we'd accidentally stumbled into a boutique staffed by magicians and overnight it had been transformed into a 7-Eleven.

Shocking. But not uncommon. In my work I see this messaging tragedy on a daily basis. Sales teams struggling to communicate the fascinating story of the solution they represent. Agents who miss the mark trying to effectively engage potential customers. Companies whose cultures wither instead of thrive because their leaders can't articulate the stories of why they do what they do.

The good news is, no amount of wizardry is required to solve this problem. In the pages that follow, we'll discover how storytelling has the power to change how everyone in business thinks, feels, and behaves, and how you can use that power yourself.

And though I highly recommend Ljubljana during the holidays, no trip to Slovenia is required.

PART ONE

The Irresistible Power
of Storytelling

CHAPTER ONE

The Gaps in Business and the Bridges That Close (and Don't Close) Them

The shortest distance between a human being and the truth is a story.

—ANTHONY DE MELLO

The cutest boy in my high school was Andy K. Truthfully, he'd been the cutest boy since third grade. No one was really sure why. Maybe because he was born in May, but his parents waited to put him in school until the following fall, so he was the oldest. Or maybe it was because he was an incredible athlete. Or simply because he just seemed slightly indifferent about everything.

3

Whatever it was, it meant the fall afternoon of my freshman year, when Andy offered to share a can of Welch's grape soda with me, my high school fate was sealed. Andy thought I was okay, which meant everyone else had to as well.

That was 1994. Social acceptance was measured that way, by the things you shared with others. Best friend heart necklaces split down the middle, cans of soda, and the other standout: packs of Extra gum.

I remember never leaving home without a pack of neon green Extra gum (thirty individually foil-wrapped pieces held loosely together with a strip of white paper). You could slip the pieces one by one from the pack, leaving a slight trace of where each had been. It was perfect for sharing with friends and boys who were slightly out of your league. Each empty pack was a symbol of social currency.

Apparently, I wasn't the only one who swore by Extra gum. For years, this Wrigley brand sat at the top of the chewable breath-freshening totem pole. Checking out at the grocery store? Grab a pack of Extra. Upcoming dentist appointment? Don't forget the Extra. It was the go-to brand and dominated the market until suddenly . . . it didn't.

By 2013, almost twenty years after my freshman year of high school when I'd never have considered buying anything *but* Extra gum, the iconic brand had slid to third position. Even as I, once a brand loyalist, glanced at the rows of gum options, Extra didn't even register with me.

Before you start feeling bad for Extra, and especially before you start thinking this was of their own doing—that they must have made an outrageously obvious, foolishly unfortunate, inevitable mistake—let's be clear: this is a fundamental problem in business. Not just for Extra. Not just for products that sit on a shelf. It's a problem in *all* business.

Ultimately, what Extra was struggling with, what all businesses struggle with, was bridging a gap.

The Gap in Your Business

The goal of a business is to profitably deliver value to people, to get a product or service from point A (the business) to point B (the people who will use it). That's it. There are an infinite number of ways to achieve these goals, of course, but the overall goal itself is pretty simple.

Simple but not easy. No goal worth attaining comes without obstacles, and in business there are plenty of those. How do you get people to buy? To invest? How do you attract talent? Retain it? How do you convince one department to act in a timely manner regarding an issue that is only relevant to another department? How do you convince a higher-up to buy in on an idea? Rally direct reports around a particular initiative? How do you get suppliers to deliver on time?

No matter where you turn, behind every corner and from every angle, there are always obstacles. In fact, getting past them is what defines successful business.

I find it more helpful, however, to think of those obstacles in business not as daunting, immovable blockages but rather as gaps. It is the space between what you want and where you are. The gap.

The most obvious gap in business is the void between the customer and the company. How does a company get its product or service into the hands of the people who need it? When you're standing in line at the grocery checkout and faced with twenty different gum options, how does Extra get you to choose Extra?

But while the sales gap is important, there are other gaps everywhere in business. There are gaps between entrepreneurs and potential investors, between recruiters and prospective employees, between managers and employees, between leaders and executives.

To make a business work, you need to bridge the gaps.

More importantly, those who bridge the gaps best, win. If you can sell better, pitch better, recruit better, build better, create better, connect better—you win.

Bridge the gaps, win the game.

Of course, in order to do that, you need to *build* the bridge.

Which is where it all starts to fall apart.

Bad Materials, Weak Bridges

Regardless of the type of gap you face in business, you must master three main elements to have any hope of building a bridge strong enough to get your intended audience—potential customers, key team members, investors, etc.—across the great divide: attention, influence, and transformation.

First and foremost, the best bridges must capture attention and captivate the audience, so they know the bridge is there in the first place. The second element, influence, is the means by which you're able to compel the audience to take the action you desire. And third, if you don't want to have to keep bridging the same gaps over and over again, the best bridges transform the audience, creating a lasting impact and leaving the audience changed, so they never even consider returning to the other side of the bridge, thereby closing the gap forever.

Pretty straightforward, right?

The problem—the tragedy really—is that despite our best efforts and intentions, we are really bad at building bridges. We focus on just one of the elements, maybe two, but rarely all three. We talk *at* people instead of engaging *with* them. We default to what's easiest or flashiest, and as a result, our bridges are flimsy, fleeting, and sometimes downright ridiculous. But because these substandard solutions are so prevalent, we've convinced ourselves they are sufficient.

Think of all the real estate agents' faces you've seen on bus stops or all the pop-up ads you've instinctually x-ed out of or the hours of commercials you've scrolled past. For a while, back in 2016, when the *Star Wars* craze was in full swing again, there was a guy who stood outside a hair salon in my neighborhood dressed like Darth Vader and holding a blow dryer as a way to lure people in for a haircut. What does Darth Vader have to do with a hair salon? It's hard to guess, since the guy always wears a helmet, and yet there he stood.

Or consider the salesperson in front of a group of decision makers who launches into her pitch, equipped with a clicker that doubles as a laser pointer. The salesperson feels pretty confident. After all, she spent no fewer than six hours cramming every last feature, benefit, percentage, and decimal point onto the deck of eighty-nine slides for a twenty-minute presentation. I mean, the people in the room won't be able to read any of it on the screen—it's too small and cluttered—but that doesn't matter because the salesperson is planning to read it *to* them off the screen. Who could possibly say no to *that*?!

Please. This bridge is no good, and anyone who tells you it is is a liar.

Let's consider the bridges we try to build internally—the ones meant to create a healthy company culture. Perhaps you work for a company that is committed to its mission and culture, which is great. The culture is taught via a handbook. And leaders within the company often send out emails or newsletters or speak from podiums using the wording from the mission statement. Maybe it's printed on mugs. But does anyone *feel* anything about it? They know the words, but do they feel it in their bones? Does it shape their decisions and create a deep sense of commitment?

It could. But, sadly, most companies and leaders have accepted the lie that repeating the mission statement is a sufficient bridge for connecting and motivating teams. The truth is, one slight breeze—one small salary increase or perk promised by another company—and, like it says in the nursery rhyme about a certain span in London, that bridge is falling down.

That being said, I feel it's only fair to mention that, yes, it *is* possible to bridge a gap without all three essential elements—attention, influence, and transformation. And it *is* possible to use materials that are cheap and blueprints designed for instant gratification versus lasting growth. For example, I confess, I am a sucker for Instagram ads that are photos of cute workout clothes. I'll usually click on the ad and even sometimes buy it. But when people ask me about my hobbies, I have to mention taking things to the UPS Store to be returned, because I return 90 percent of my Insta-ad buys.

I doubt that's what you're going for.

I doubt you're investing in marketing only to have your products returned or forgotten. Or that you enjoy creating constant price cuts for random holidays. Or giving pitches that don't close. Or talking to employees who tune you out. Or creating social media posts no one will click on. Or implementing random contests to achieve arbitrary goals. I doubt you hire, train, and incentivize top talent just to have them look elsewhere the second you take the carrot away or offer a slightly smaller carrot.

If gaps have emerged in your business or on your path to success that you just can't seem to close, there's a good chance the problem starts with the elements you're using, or not using, to build your bridges.

The question is, what works? If none of these tactics get the job done, what does? Is there a way to simultaneously capture attention, influence, and transform audiences? How do you build bridges that last and close the gaps once and for all?

That is the very question Extra gum was desperate to answer.

The Gap-Bridging Solution

With sales in a steady slide and their once effortless title as king of the gum mountain no longer on firm footing, Extra had to do something. At first, they did what any of us would do: they went back to the basics. They went back to what worked during the Extra glory days. They doubled down on the feature Extra was known for: long-lasting flavor. You couldn't watch a sitcom in the eighties without seeing a commercial of smiling people living their best lives, while chewing the same piece of flavor-filled gum for what one could only imagine was weeks at a time.

Long-lasting flavor! That was obviously the answer. So the team at Extra created more messages about how extra Extra really was. The result was abysmal. First, it gained little if any attention (a search on YouTube for any of these commercials will leave you empty-handed) and even less influence. Sales still slid.

The gap reality remained. When it came to that critical, less-than-two-second moment in the grocery aisle when consumers might choose Extra, they didn't. Determined, Extra sought answers. They hired a research firm to determine why people buy gum in the first place and when the gum-buying decision was actually made.

The results were fascinating. It turns out 95 percent of gum decisions are made unconsciously, without the consumer even knowing it.[1] This meant, in order to be the gap winner when the zombie buyer reached for a breath-freshening solution, Extra had to somehow burrow itself into the depths of the human psyche. They had to exist in that special place where logic doesn't really matter. A place where gum buying was about more than just buying gum; it was connected to the human experience.

Essentially, Extra needed to get consumers across the bridge.

But how? And was it even possible with something as commoditized as chewing gum?

The answer that worked for Extra is the same answer that will work for you. No matter the scenario. No matter the gap. No matter the product or the audience. The easiest, most effective way to build bridges that capture attention, influence behavior, and transform those who cross them, resulting in gaps that stay closed and bridges that last, is with storytelling.

In the end, stories are what stick.

Storytelling and Building Bridges That Last

Before we continue, let me clarify something. While this book is about storytelling in business, that is not where my experience with the power of storytelling began. I didn't work at a marketing firm or on a sales team and *then* discover the power of stories.

My experience *started* with storytelling. Business was an afterthought.

As I said earlier, I told my first story when I was eleven years old. It was an assignment for my fifth-grade English class. I continued telling stories for entertainment at my church and then on the speech team in high school. After graduation, I attended and told stories at storytelling festivals across the country. I attended storytelling workshops, retreats, and conferences. I sat at the feet of storytelling masters who, without any agenda, could captivate audiences of hundreds. Storytellers who could take small moments and give them big meaning, with nothing but the command of their narrative.

It was there, in the presence of story and storytelling in its purest form, that I first witnessed its irresistible power: a power that effortlessly includes all three of the bridge-building elements of attention, influence, and transformation.

Storytelling and Attention

I recently enjoyed a lunch with marketing executives in higher education. They were lamenting the abysmal attention span of their customers, namely, seventeen-year-olds, and it appeared as though my suggestion to tell better stories instead of focusing on using the fewest words possible was causing some internal chaos. One gentleman, tempering his frustration, asked, "So how do you suggest we incorporate a long-form story when our audience has an attention span shorter than a goldfish?"

The question was a good one but flawed. First, the whole goldfish thing, if you've heard it before, is a myth.

Second, it implied the message recipient was at fault, conveniently shifting the blame away from the message creator. Maybe people don't pay attention because your hashtags don't matter IRL (in real life).

Finally, and most importantly, the question revealed the subtle belief that the marketer's relationship with an audience's attention has to be a challenged one. But, in fact, when done correctly, attention doesn't have to be stolen or wrestled away. It is given. Freely, willingly, and in many cases, without the audience realizing it's happening.

This ease of attention is one of the great strengths of storytelling and is the result of a unique leverage point no other form of information exchange has: the storytelling process is a co-creative one. As the teller tells the story, the listener is taking the words and adding their own images and emotions to them. Yes, the story is about certain characters in a certain setting, but listeners will fill in the narrative with their own experiences until the lines between the message and the recipients are blurred. Researchers have explored this aspect of storytelling, calling the experience of losing oneself in a story "narrative transportation"[2] and even claiming one of the negative aspects of storytelling is, when we are truly transported into a story, we lose awareness of our immediate surroundings.[3] If you've ever missed your exit while listening to a story-driven podcast or audiobook, you understand these effects all too well. And think about it. In that moment, did you feel coerced into surrendering your attention? No. You traveled willingly into the world of the story. And it is at this point that attention metamorphizes into something much more valuable: captivation.

Captivate your audience with a story and, much like I found in the Slovenian boutique, you will have access to all the attention you could ever need.

Storytelling and Influence

In addition to the captivating effects of a story, or more accurately, as a result of them, stories possess an inherent persuasive quality. Researchers have tested this as well, determining that, as audiences lose themselves in a story, their attitudes change to reflect the story minus the typical scrutiny.[4] (More on that scrutiny in chapter 4.)

With story, resistance dissipates. With story, we don't need to taste the food to want to go to the restaurant or smell the cologne to want to buy a bottle. A story allows people to fall in love with the product, appreciate the value of the service, and feel compelled to act. When the Slovenian clerk started to tell us the Eight & Bob story, we didn't feel sold or convinced. We were willing participants and acted of our own desire. Which, I don't know about you, seems like a much more desirable way to cross a bridge.

11

Storytelling and Transformation

We know that story has an ability to transport the listener into the world of that story (attention). We know the more engrossed an audience is in a story, the more likely they are to adopt the perspectives within the story (influence). And for the final element, research has also determined that, once an audience emerges from the story, they are changed.[5] And not just for a minute or two; the effects are long-lasting.[6]

Have you ever left a movie theater and felt like the story followed you home and stayed with you for a while? Have you ever heard a story from a friend that weaves itself into the fiber of your being? I once shared a story with two friends about a girl I knew who lost her baby daughter in a tragic drowning accident. My friends still comment they will never forget that story, and now they drain their kiddie pools after every use.

This kind of lasting impact is not reserved for Hollywood and tragedies; it is inherent in all well-told stories. The Eight & Bob story did more than just convert; it turned Michael and me into converts. We were transformed by the story. We couldn't wait to tell it. To share it. We became like the sales clerk who had been just bursting to tell us the story. The desire to share it was as urgent and contagious as a cough and lasted much longer.

A story's transformative power can also extend beyond the recipient. Sometimes a story can transform the message itself. The task of bridging the gaps in business can appear to be transactional, with the goal being simply to get customers and stakeholders from point A to point B. It's easy to get caught up in the day-to-day functions and responsibilities, to lose touch with the bigger, more noble cause beneath it all, which—call me an optimist—I believe is always there, no matter how dry the work may seem to be. Refocusing the message on that noble cause taps into the transformative power of storytelling.

I once worked with a transit company whose sole purpose was moving things from here to there, but they understood their work as being about helping customers keep their promises. Noble.

I've also worked with title companies who, on the surface, may appear to be the soulless *i*-dotters and *t*-crossers of the mortgage and home-buying process. But as they understood it, their work is what makes the American dream possible and allows people to confidently call a home their own. Noble.

In business, there is always more than meets the eye, something bigger at play. Telling the story of that something can transform business entirely.

And telling that something-bigger story is exactly what Extra gum decided to do.

Extra Gum and the Ultimate Story Bridge

After extensive research and investment in consumer analytics, Extra knew without a doubt that in that critical two-second window in the checkout line most gum purchases were unconsciously made. In order to be the gum of choice, Extra had to connect with consumers in a real and visceral way long before they found themselves in the grocery aisle. Highlighting standard one-dimensional, nonemotional features like long-lasting flavor weren't enough to bridge the gap, so they decided to go bigger.

Through more research, they discovered one of the deeper, driving emotions for gum purchasing was the "social aspect of sharing it with others."[7] This isn't only true for gum; other breath-freshening options such as Tic Tac and Altoids also focus their product design to encourage sharing: a win-win. The mint owners gain social points for generosity, and the mint makers sell more mints. Essentially, just like a freight company is about more than moving things from place to place and title agencies are about more than stacks of papers and getting signatures, gum, if you choose to see it as such—and more importantly, choose to *sell* it as such—is about more than long-lasting flavor.

Gum is about togetherness, closeness, and connection, all of which are pretty important to the human experience. If Extra could find a way to tap into that emotion, when their customers stared blankly at rows of gum, a flash of that greater meaning would cross their minds, connect them to Extra, and lead to a sale.

In 2015, Extra launched a two-minute video about a boy and a girl, Juan and Sarah, but the names didn't really matter. The gum didn't even really matter. What mattered was the story.

The video opened with a scene outside a high school. We catch a glimpse of Sarah. She is pretty in that "girl next door" kind of way, and while the camera focuses on her face, she smiles slightly. In the next frame we see why she's smiling, or rather who she is smiling at, namely, Juan, a handsome young man with kind eyes. He smiles back.

Moments later, we see Sarah at her locker and she drops all of her books. As fate would have it, Juan is there and helps pick them up for her. As a thank you, Sarah offers him a piece of Extra gum. It's one of the only times we see the gum in the video.

As the two minutes play out, we see Juan and Sarah's relationship evolve through several vignettes: their first kiss in the front seat of Juan's car, their first argument, the two of them falling in love the way high school kids do. Then we see Sarah at an airport. She's leaving. We see Sarah in a high-rise office in an unnamed city. Suddenly, like Dorothy and Kansas, we realize we're not in high school anymore. This is real life, and the glow from the beginning of the video is gone. It all feels cold as Sarah and Juan try to connect via video chat.

If you look up this video on YouTube and hover your cursor over the time bar at the bottom of the screen at this point in the video, you would see there isn't much time left for these two to figure it out. You would also notice it didn't take much time for you to care about them figuring it out. But we'll get to that later.

With only a few seconds remaining, the scene shifts. Sarah is walking into an empty space. An abandoned art gallery, maybe? A restaurant with no tables? We don't know. Sarah seems confused too.

She looks around and notices a series of small framed pictures on the wall. She walks up to the first one. It's a sketch of a boy helping a girl pick up her books in front of a locker. Sarah smiles. We smile.

In the next frame is a sketch of a boy kissing a girl in the front seat of his car.

As Sarah passes each picture, we realize these are sketches of moments in Juan and her relationship, and we are reminded of the beautiful love Sarah and Juan shared.

Wait! Reminded? It's only been seventy seconds. That's barely enough time to process, much less be reminded of anything. And yet a sense of nostalgia washes over us. Nostalgia for Juan and Sarah or maybe our own love stories. They seem to blend together.

Sarah eventually comes to the end of the row of sketches.

I hold my breath as she steps closer to the final sketch.

Her eyes widen. It's a picture of a boy on one knee, holding a ring, proposing to the girl.

But wait! That doesn't make sense. Juan hasn't propo—

Our unconscious minds trail off, our jaws drop, our eyes burn as Sarah turns around to see Juan on one knee, holding a ring. They embrace and the video flashes back to that first exchange: a slight smile from a pretty girl to a kind boy. And now, here they are.

I've seen this video many times. It's pretty much required when you're writing a chapter whose arc is wrapped around this story within a story. That being said, the video gets me every time I watch it.

In fact, I am writing these words right now at thirty thousand feet on a connecting flight. I signed onto the Wi-Fi on my computer and cued up the video. Not really thinking about it, I pressed play and was immediately transported into Juan and Sarah's world. Two minutes later, I had tears streaming down my cheeks and sniffed uncontrollably. (Typically, I'd feel self-conscious, wondering what the person sitting next to me must be thinking about the weeping person in 7A. But on this particular flight the guy sitting next to me is an aggressive leg shaker and has been rattling the entire row for the past two hours, so I figure we're even.)

It's also important to note, because I'd recently switched to an iPhone X, I didn't have any headphones that are compatible with my laptop on this flight. So I was forced to watch the video of Juan and Sarah on mute.

I mention this because some might argue, after watching the video, that it is the music that makes the story so compelling. But even as a silent film, the story struck a nerve in me. There was something about the unfolding of Juan and Sarah's story that brought me back. Watching it, I was suddenly a freshman in high school and remembering the thrill and the innocence and the beauty of when Andy K. handed me that can of grape soda and smiled. Though our story didn't end in a proposal, the emotional stirring via a vicarious trip down memory lane is exactly what Extra was going for and overwhelmingly achieved.

It might be important for me to remind you at this moment that this story, this Juan and Sarah thing, was actually about gum. That thing you mindlessly buy and haphazardly chew. That thing that Extra, if it wanted to affect net-positive sales, had to connect to your emotions in order to interrupt your unconscious purchasing habits. So how do you emotionally connect people to gum? You tell them a story. The story of Juan and Sarah. And you subtly drop your product into the story. A piece of gum shared at the beginning and—oh, I forgot to mention it, because I barely noticed it—all of the sketches in that final scene are drawn on the inside of Extra foil wrappers. Yes, gum is there. But the story is about so much more.

When you tell a story, it always is.

Extra took the original video and created a variety of fifteen-, thirty-, and sixty-second versions. Since they knew the two-minute version would be the most impactful, they launched a significant digital ad campaign around the long version so that when the shorter versions were released on television, many viewers would have already seen the whole story.

The response was everything Extra could have hoped for: tweets, retweets, and Facebook posts, oh my! Ellen DeGeneres tweeted about it, and YouTube viewers voted it as the ad of the year in the "Gives You the Feels" category.

While we all want social love, and likes, shares, comments and retweets are nice, what Extra was most concerned with was bridging the sales gap. The success of this campaign was measured entirely on whether or not people purchased packs of Extra gum. At the critical moment—the moment of gap-closing truth—did consumers *buy* Extra?

The answer? Yes, they did.

The two-minute video has been viewed over one hundred million times, and more importantly, Extra reversed their declining sales.[8]

Now *that* is a happily-ever-after if ever there was one.

From Why to How

The benefits of storytelling are compelling and real, and they, in effect, answer the why of this book. Storytelling is one of the most powerful business-building tools in existence. It captivates, influences, and transforms customers, stakeholders, talent, and beyond, closing the gaps in business with bridges that last.

But how is that so? How is it that something as simple as a story can be so powerful in business? To understand that, and to start the process of finding and telling your own stories, we need to travel to the source of where stories begin in the teller and the place where they find their home in the receiver: the brain.

CHAPTER TWO

Once Upon a Brain

Storyhacking the Nervous System to Captivate, Influence, and Transform

> *Story is the language of the brain.*
> —LISA CRON, *STORY GENIUS*

I n the summer of 2014, the Maricopa Medical Center was in a bind. This was, to be clear, nothing new. County- and district-level hospitals are almost *always* in a bind. Not all hospitals are created equal, and if you run a county hospital in the United States, there's a good chance you're at the low end of the food chain, where binds are prevalent.

The issue comes down to demographics. If you're wealthy and well insured or have solid coverage from your place of work, a county hospital is not usually your first choice for treatment. If you're in a low-income bracket with little to no healthcare coverage or uninsured, a county hospital is often your only choice. Maricopa, like most county hospitals, is a health-care safety net.

For all its county status, however, the Maricopa Medical Center in Maricopa, Arizona, has a remarkable reputation. For the nearly twenty thousand patients a year coming through its doors, there are numerous specialists and specialized units, including the second-busiest burn center in the country, which has a patient survival rate of more than 97 percent. As Arizona's oldest teaching hospital, Maricopa is noted for cultivating incredible physicians every year. By almost any measure, Maricopa defies its small-scale, county status; it's busy, inspiring, and nationally recognized for excellence.

But like every county health-care facility, it's also on a never-ending quest for cash. After all, it's hard to be a safety net for a community that is mostly poor and be flush at the same time.

Enter the Maricopa Health Foundation (MHF). While the hospital itself works to win public funds, the MHF's job is to raise private funds to support it. As part of that mission, MHF holds an annual fund-raising dinner called the Copa Ball. It's an important part of the foundation's efforts. But fund-raising in 2014 was worrisome.

Fund-raising for county hospitals is, by default, challenging. Unlike raising money for an arts foundation or a high-profile charity, the people who frequent the hospital, and therefore would be most likely to financially support it, are there because they don't have access to excess funds. Anytime the people who *use* a service aren't the ones who help *pay* for the service, fund-raising can get tough.

The previous year, the foundation had tried to address this by having physicians take the stage and talk about their work. The doctors spoke about the urgent nature of their work and how importantly they needed technology A or critical equipment B. At the end, the audience was asked to give a financial donation to the foundation.

Since the audience held a number of medical and local professionals, the doctor presentations seemed like a good bet. Credibility? Check. Connection? Check. But *financial* checks? Not so much. The fund-raiser worked, but it fell short of what the foundation had hoped to raise.

This year there was an additional fund-raising challenge: a nearly billion-dollar funding bond was up for a vote in the state. In a conservative state, the bond was not wildly popular. Only top-notch marketing efforts and nonstop grassroots initiatives would get the votes needed to pass the bond. Of course, top-notch marketing and nonstop anything requires a lot of money. Which meant the people sitting in the ballroom the night of the 2014 Copa Ball had already been asked, on numerous occasions, to give money to support the bond marketing initiatives. Which subsequently meant whoever took the stage that year would be speaking to six hundred people who were already financially tapped out and weary of being asked.

———

When I met with the MHF, I was particularly concerned with the first problem: the gap between the predominantly low-income users and the predominantly high-income potential donors. The challenge, as I saw it, wasn't to simply convince people to part with their money by making a more convincing argument about how important things were. That was a rational appeal, but one that seemed doomed to be a repeat of the previous year's lackluster results.

The people attending the Copa Ball, I explained, weren't short on caring. And contrary to common belief, they weren't short on cash—people will always give to causes they care about. What the foundation needed to do was to close the gap between the donors and the hospital. We needed to make the donors see they weren't only funding an impersonal entity; they were funding *their* hospital, a hospital they cared about.

That, I knew, was a gap made for bridging through story, because as the MHF would soon discover, story has a unique place in the human brain.

Blubbering at Forty Thousand Feet: How Story Runs the Brain

Chick flicks are out.

That's what Paul Zak had told his bride some six years earlier. Take a girlfriend to those movies, not him. Give him prison or boxing flicks, Stallone or Schwarzenegger, not Nicholas Sparks.[1] But things changed on a late flight home to California, where, as Zak, a neuroscientist, articulated it, he "discovered that I am the last person you would want sitting next to you on a plane."

Exhausted after a five-day stint in Washington, DC, Zak ditched work and his laptop in favor of the tough-guy, Clint Eastwood–directed, award-winning film *Million Dollar Baby*. At the climax of the movie, Zak began to cry. And it wasn't just crying; it was uncontrollable weeping, or, as he described it, "heaving big sloppy sobs."[2]

In his work, Zak is credited with the discovery that oxytocin, a tiny neurochemical made in the hypothalamus of mammal brains, is more than just the bonding chemical for mothers and children. He showed it is synthesized in the brain by trust and that it motivates reciprocity. Oxytocin, he proved, is basically a prosocial chemical. It helps us bond, trust, and love. In fact, his work earned him the nickname "Dr. Love." After his dramatic experience on the plane, Dr. Love began to wonder if the brain releases oxytocin when we watch movies? Is that why we cry?

To find out, Zak worked with a group of graduate students to design an experiment in which subjects watched a video from a children's hospital. In it, a father talks about his two-year-old son, Ben, who has terminal brain cancer.

"The story has a classic dramatic arc," Zak wrote, "in which the father is struggling to connect to and enjoy his son, all the while knowing that the child has only a few months to live. The clip concludes with the father finding the strength to stay emotionally close to his son 'until he takes his last breath.'"[3]

Needless to say, the video is an intensely emotional story.

Another group also watched a video of Ben and his father, but one in which they spend a day at the zoo. It's touching in its own way but without the dramatic emotional pull of the first clip. Where the first is a story, the second is more descriptive coverage.

Zak's team measured oxytocin in the blood in both groups before and after the video and found that those who watched the first video—the one with the story—had a 47 percent increase in oxytocin.

It's what happened after, though, that matters for business. That's when oxytocin began to change behavior. Those who watched the first video were more generous toward others and gave more to a cancer charity. Story, in other words, made people better connected, more trusting, and generous.

But First, Attention . . .

Of course, you can't make any kind of impact on people unless you get their attention. You have to captivate in order to influence. You can't gain trust if no one sees you in the first place.

Story has us covered here too.

In further experiments, Zak noted that people who watched public service announcements increased their donations to charity by 261 percent when their oxytocin and cortisol (which is correlated with attention) increased.[4] Just one factor alone wasn't enough to get those results: you needed both attention *and* trust.

What Zak had shown in the lab was the neurological basis for what storytellers have known for ages: stories focus your attention and forge bonds, based in trust, between people. In essence, Zak's research showed how story placed people at the intersection of captivation and influence.

Once you've caught people's attention with a little cortisol and once you have trust, thanks to oxytocin, people become more giving. But you don't need to drag people into a lab and dose them with neurochemicals to influence their behavior. You just have to tell them stories. And that's exactly what MHF chose to do.

Storyhacking Charity

The format for the Copa Ball is like many charity events. A speaker delivers a short speech and then there's an ask, a request for donations. The checkbooks or smartphones with giving apps come out, and then another speaker takes the stage. It's like a small telethon, where performers do their bit and the host asks for donations.

This is an effective model only if the speakers deliver. My job was to convince MHF that simply having speakers endorse a cause and emphasize its importance wasn't enough. As in Paul Zak's studies, the key to more donations lay in using story to change minds and hearts, to increase attention and trust and, through that, generosity. Logic and credibility and rhetoric, I explained, weren't going to make the cause any more important than they had the year before. By using stories, though, we could hack the very neurology that connects people at a fundamental level and drives trust and generosity.

After meeting with the foundation, I suggested they should fill the speaking slate based on what kind of stories needed to be told rather than choose speakers solely by pedigree. Instead of choosing the people first, I suggested, choose the stories.

Armed with some story ideas in mind, the foundation went looking for speakers. And they found exactly what they needed, which, as it turned out, wasn't doctors. Instead, that year's speaking lineup at the Copa Ball included a former secretary of state, a young man who'd had serious facial reconstruction at the hospital, and a prominent local luminary.

As with the previous year, each person had credibility. They were a potential social and demographic match for the donors who would be at the event. But this year, the speakers had something even better: they had stories. For the next few weeks I met with each of them to help capture and craft their stories for the Copa Ball.

When the evening of the ball arrived, I stood anxiously at the back of the room, nervous for the speakers but excited to have the sellout crowd of six hundred experience the same stories I'd heard and nurtured.

The first speaker of the evening had been a patient of the hospital years earlier. He was in his early twenties when he intervened in a bar fight with terrible consequences. He was severely beaten, his face was crushed, and an orbital socket was broken.

When he arrived at Maricopa, it was clear he needed immediate surgery. There was just one problem: he had no insurance. Reconstructive surgery is prohibitively expensive. For an uninsured person barely out of high school, his ability to pay was essentially impossible. He would have to go through life disfigured.

The man explained how he told the doctor he had no insurance and couldn't possibly afford the surgery. "The doctor just put his hand on my shoulder," he recalled, "and said, 'We've got your back.'"

That night, under the stage lights or even up close, there was no way to see the steel plates the doctors at the Maricopa Medical Center had carefully placed beneath the skin of this handsome man's face. But everyone could see the slight mist that covered his eyes as he told a spellbound audience what it was like to know that, when you need it most, more than you ever will in your whole life, someone has your back.

When the ask happened, the response was overwhelming.

Betsey Bayless was the next speaker. A former secretary of state for Arizona, she carried plenty of credibility. She was also the former chief executive officer for the Maricopa Integrated Health System (MIHS), which was another challenge. It would be far too tempting and feel much safer for her to revert to a rhetoric she knew all too well: high-level corporate speak about the important work the hospital did and why it was so critical to give. But Secretary Bayless took the road less traveled and instead told a story, not as a former CEO or former secretary of state, but as a daughter.

Some years earlier, her father had a stroke. He needed immediate care. She didn't call the paramedics because she knew they'd take him to the closest hospital—an upscale, private facility. Instead, Secretary Bayless transferred her father from a wheelchair into her car and made the harrowing journey to Maricopa Medical Center.

"When we got there," Bayless recounted, "the doctor was waiting at the curb. When someone you love needs help, needs it desperately, you can't imagine how it feels to know that, at Maricopa, someone will be waiting there for you."

Once again, the audience responded emotionally and with donations.

The last speaker was Marilyn Seymann. A PhD with a decades-long career in finance and government, Marilyn was a well-known, well-respected Phoenix treasure. Her message, however, wasn't the standard lofty plea to give. Instead, Marilyn shared a personal story about the day she was strolling with a friend and was hit by a car. Unable to respond in the ambulance, she was not taken to the hospital of her choosing but to the closest one, which was the Maricopa Medical Center.

Marilyn told the story of the incredible care the physicians gave her. When it came time for the third ask of the night, the audience all but threw money onto the stage.

The evening was a phenomenal success. There was no shortage of tears, laughter, and goodwill. Just as it had reduced Paul Zak to tears at 40,000 feet, story had delivered an oxytocin current of connective emotion throughout the crowd. People were captivated by the stories of loss, hope, and redemption. The audience connected with the people telling the stories in a way they never had in the history of the Copa Ball.

In fact, it's not unreasonable to say that it was more than a simple connection, but instead a powerful synchronization. As Uri Hasson, a

Princeton neuroscientist, has shown, the brains of storytellers and story listeners can synchronize.[5] Stories don't just make us like each other; they make us *like* each other. They make us similar. Paul Zak observed, "If you pay attention to the story and become emotionally engaged with the story's characters, then it is as if you have been transported into the story's world. This is why your palms sweat when James Bond dodges bullets. And why you stifle a sniffle when Bambi's mother dies."[6]

Even without the action of James Bond and the impossible cuteness of Bambi, the Copa Ball tapped into the same brain processes. When the proceeds were tallied, the donations were more than double those of the previous year.

Lasting Change

The stories from that night's speakers were the bridge the organization needed. But even Paul Zak was a little confused in his study by how well storytelling elicited donations. "If you think about it," he wrote, "the donations are quite odd. . . . The money donated to charity cannot help these actors out of their fictional binds. . . . Nevertheless, oxytocin makes people want to help others in costly and tangible ways."[7]

What Zak was speaking of is the lasting effect of story, that is, the third part of effective bridge building, namely, the transformation that occurs from changes in the brain. Oxytocin in the brain, which is elicited by story, also activates another circuit called HOME (human oxytocin-mediated empathy). Among other things, that circuit uses dopamine, which is a reinforcement neurochemical. And dopamine helps us learn by giving us a little jolt every time something notable happens.

In other words, story can create lasting impacts because we remember better when we hear stories. This is one of the most compelling attributes of storytelling. Go back to a time before computer storage. Go back to a time before photographs, books, and even the written word, and you will find stories, told verbally and handed down from generation to generation. Why? Because they were memorable. They lasted. A lesson taught in story was a lesson that could be recalled when it mattered.

A lesson learned can make all the difference in the evolution of a species. Or the life of a hospital. Because stories captivate and influence the brain, but they also transform it.

Or as Zak so eloquently put it, "The narrative is over, but the effects linger."[8]

Not Just Any Story . . .

There's one catch in all of this.

For all the power of story to captivate, influence, and transform the brain, there are two key things we also know from studying the neural impact of story. The first is that there actually has to be a story. If you've ever been to a conference, a Monday morning meeting, or anything involving PowerPoint slides and a lot of text, you know that not everything is a story.

Second, not all stories are created equal.

Some stories suck.

Actually, a lot of stories suck.

This is, in essence, the lesson that neurology teaches us about the brain and business: you have to use stories *and* they have to be good ones.

Which leaves us here: what exactly *is* a story and how do you tell a great one?

CHAPTER THREE

What Makes a Story Great

(And Beats Puppies and Supermodels Every Time)

The power of storytelling is exactly this: to bridge the gaps where everything else has crumbled.
—PAULO COELHO

My grandma on my dad's side was a huge sports fan. Even as her mind failed her, she could remember the names and stats for every player on both the Minnesota Twins and Vikings teams. Eventually, she barely recognized her grandchildren, but she could still pick out a player by the way he walked on the field.

Sundays with my grandma were my first introduction to football. Years later, when Michael and I were dating, he preferred spending Sundays

29

on the couch watching football too. To keep me from convincing him otherwise, Michael started telling me the drama behind the game. The trades, the grudges, the betrayals, the underdogs. As soon as I knew the stories, you couldn't pull me away if you wanted to. And trust me, there were moments when Michael wanted to. Apparently, yelling at the television is only appropriate at certain moments of the game, not the whole time. "That's what you get, Tony Romo, for dumping Jessica Simpson!" "Saints?! Saints?! What kind of a name is that?! I think they'll see you in hell for that shot at Favre." I even lost my voice and nearly got into a fight during Super Bowl XLIII, when the Cardinals were playing the Steelers.

What can I say? It's easy for me to get wrapped up in the tragedy and triumph of a great game. And I'm not alone. For Super Bowls, a good chunk of the nation gets involved in the drama. And if you happen to be the gambling type, that drama hits a whole new level.

The 2014 Super Bowl between the Seattle Seahawks and the Denver Broncos was a tough one for gamblers. Two-thirds of them wagered on the Broncos that day—a choice that turned out to be an expensive mistake. In what would become the worst day for gamblers in Super Bowl history,[1] Seattle crushed Denver and won the forty-eighth Super Bowl in one of the greatest upsets in the game's history. Denver, meanwhile, would set their own record for being the only team in the previous three decades to score less than ten points in a Super Bowl. Ouch.

For the majority of gamblers across America, the game was a disaster. But while the odds makers may have gotten the game itself wrong, one man managed to make a bet that *did* come true: he accurately predicted which ad would be the favorite of the 2014 broadcast.

What's $4 Million Between Friends?

The Super Bowl is a marketing phenomenon. Over a third of Americans watch the game in any given year—a staggering number. For sheer eyeballs alone, it's an advertiser's dream. But the Super Bowl has some special mojo that other broadcast events don't: people actually want to see the commercials.

Crazy but true. If you've ever been to a Super Bowl party, you've experienced the bizarre phenomenon firsthand. It's one of the only moments in television when viewers get quieter when the ads come on.

For advertisers, the combination of total eyeballs and focused attention is marketing nirvana. Not only do Super Bowl ads get more attention than other ads—experts begin a running commentary weeks before the actual game—but brands get a certain marketing cred just for showing up. A Super Bowl spot gives companies and their anointed ad firms a cachet that can't be bought.

Except, of course, it *can* be bought. That's the point. And in 2014, the ads were running at a record-high $4 million per thirty-second spot.

Even with all those eyeballs, that's a high price tag when there really isn't clear evidence that Super Bowl ads lead to sales. Volkswagen claimed to get $100 million in free publicity from its admittedly awesome ad featuring a kid dressed as Darth Vader[2] (yes, sometimes a Darth Vader costume can work in a brand's favor), but calculating return is tricky at best. And even if you can do the math, an ad in the big game is still a gamble. Get it wrong, and you lose millions of dollars. More importantly, get it really wrong, and you lose face in front of a hundred million people. As with the oddsmakers, for the advertisers of the world, the Super Bowl is one big bet.

No doubt these things were on more than a few minds at Anheuser-Busch when they were making the ad "Puppy Love" for the 2014 Super Bowl. In addition to the standard high stakes, the brand also had a reputation to protect. Their Clydesdale-themed Super Bowl ads were perennial hits, nailing down a place in Ad Meter's Top Five more times than any other brand the previous decade.

That alone made the upcoming ad a good bet for favorite. There was no doubt Anheuser-Busch would be pulling out all the stops. And if you dig into the ad, there are a lot of reasons to point to why anyone might think it would be a winner.[3]

First, it's insanely cute. I mean, it's centered around a Labrador puppy for heaven's sake. Beyond cute, though, the spot was directed by Jake Scott, son of famed director Ridley Scott, who, interestingly, directed the famous Apple "1984" ad that aired in Super Bowl XVIII. The humans in front of the camera, meanwhile, include a gorgeous former swimsuit model and actress and a handsome, rugged man. And then there was the song playing behind it all: the beautiful "Let Her Go" by British musician Passenger.

In short, there were a lot of great reasons to think the ad would score.

None of those, however, were what made Johns Hopkins marketing professor and researcher Keith Quesenberry think the ad would be a winner. He accurately predicted in advance that the ad would be a favorite, not because it featured cute puppies and hot humans, but because it used a story.[4]

All Hail Storytelling

Now, you're obviously reading a book about storytelling, and the kind of person who buys a book about storytelling is probably the kind of person who believes in the power of a story or, at the very least, is intrigued by the idea. And because you are either intrigued or invested in what a story is capable of, you are likely not surprised by the statement above: a commercial would be picked to win because it tells a story.

But this casual acceptance of story is the very source of the bridge-building, gap-closing problem we discussed in chapter 1. Storytelling has become a do-no-wrong term, a cure-all elixir, and as a result no one challenges it. Telling a story is obviously the answer.

It might surprise you to learn this is new, this blind acceptance of storytelling. Very, very new.

In December 2004, a full decade before the 2014 Super Bowl, the only thing that stood between me and going home for a one-month break was my master's thesis initial defense meeting.

It's much worse than it sounds.

As a graduate student, you spend the first half of the year collecting and analyzing research and then writing a twenty-page preliminary paper on an idea you want to test in the second semester. The defense is a meeting with the key professors in your department who, for no less than an hour, drill you on your research and the idea you want to test. Do well in the initial defense and you're given a blessing to continue. Do poorly? It's your academic time-of-death.

My thesis examined the role of storytelling in organizational socialization. I wanted to determine what role, for better or for worse, stories played in building the culture of a company. Today, this topic wouldn't raise an eyebrow. Everyone is exploring company culture, and storytelling is generally accepted as something that happens or should happen or is happening. But in 2004 that wasn't the case.

I don't remember what I wore. I don't remember everyone who sat in that room. But I'll never forget the thickness of the air as I took my place at the head of the boardroom table. One of the professors, my thesis advisor, welcomed and thanked the rest of the attending faculty, but before she could even motion to, much less mention, the grocery-store pastries we had provided, one of the professors said, "I disagree with the premise of your thesis."

I didn't watch much *ER*, but even I knew this was the equivalent of the ominous moment when the beeping oscilloscope turned into a steady, alarming, one-tone sound. She's flatlined! The patient is dead. Cue sad music.

The room was silent. Everyone stared across the pastries at me. The professor continued, reading directly from the document I had spent weeks, yes, but also a lifetime writing.

"Humans are storytelling creatures by nature." No, he mocked.

"Cultures use stories to make sense and create shared meaning." No, he said.

I spent the next hour fighting for storytelling, for its validity, for its role in our lives, in our work, in what it means to be human. That it is a phenomenon worth studying, a skill worth investing in. I posited that we tell stories to remember. We tell them to cooperate. We tell them to entertain. We tell stories to teach, to share, and to survive.

The fact that we homo sapiens are the evolutionary winners in the race to still exist is *because* of our ability to tell each other stories. Our ability to tell stories is what enabled us to "not merely imagine things, but to do so collectively." These are the words of Yuval Noah Harari in his 2015 *New York Times* bestselling book *Sapiens*. It only took 24 pages of the 443 for him to mention storytelling.

"The ability to speak about fictions is the most unique feature of Sapien languages . . . such myths give Sapiens the unprecedented ability to cooperate flexibly in large numbers," which means we "can cooperate in extremely flexible ways with countless numbers of strangers."

Harari admitted, "Telling effective stories is not easy. . . . Yet when it succeeds, it gives Sapiens immense power, because it enables millions of strangers to cooperate and work towards common goals. Just try to imagine how difficult it would have been to create states, or churches or legal systems if we could only speak about things that really exist, such as rivers, trees and lions."[5]

I've never met Harari. I'm hoping I'll run into him on the street someday. I've already planned what I will say: "That book was amazing. Why couldn't you have released it six years earlier?"

That is when I really could have used that book. That's when I needed the ammunition. When I was sitting in that university board-room alone, surrounded by powerful faculty who essentially held the fate of my future in their hands. They had the power to let me continue my research or send me all the way back to the beginning. Do not pass Go. Do not collect $200. And delay my life indefinitely because they didn't believe in—and I couldn't convince them of—the importance of storytelling.

I'm not sure what I said that day. Fortunately for me, whatever it was, it was good enough, and I was allowed to continue to pursue my thesis and graduate on time.

Though I was the only one in the room fighting for the efficacy of a thesis on storytelling that December day, ask any early twenty-first-century storytelling advocate, and they'll tell you the value of storytelling, particularly in business, was once a tough thing to defend. It shouldn't have been, but it was. The general consensus then was that more information meant better decision making. The secret to making business work was to give consumers or team members or people more options and more information about those options.

Business was all about logic.

And then suddenly it wasn't.

The Story Emperor Has No Clothes

Several years ago, I was sitting in a neighborhood coffee shop, MacBook Pro on the table, earphones in place, trying to get some work done. But I knew better. If I really wanted to get any work done I would have gone to a library or at least a different neighborhood's coffee shop. Instead, I chatted with the dozen different people I knew from a dozen different places and accomplished nothing.

Just about the time I started to feel guilty for paying someone to watch my kids while I socialized, an acquaintance walked in. He was a commercial real estate developer I'd met through the spin studio where I worked out. We had a friendly conversation and discussed which spin classes we had (or in his case *hadn't*) attended that week. When he asked what I was working on, I mentioned storytelling. He knew this was something I was involved with and had, in fact, read some of my work.

"Actually," he said, "I just bought a book at the airport about storytelling. I think I need to become a better storyteller."

I knew the book he was talking about; there was really only one out at the time. I also knew that book wasn't going to help him much.

Sure, it used the word *storytelling* a lot. It even included examples of what most of us might think were stories. But after reading it, you'd be left with the same questions you had when you dropped the twenty-five bucks to buy it. What is a story? And how do I use one in my business and life?

When I asked what he thought of the book, he shrugged. It was all right, he said. I could tell he was disappointed, and I wasn't surprised. I remember thinking in that moment there was still a lot of work to be done on making storytelling in business more accessible. More doable.

I wish I could tell you what's changed since then. Why, in a few short years, storytelling went from something you took children to the library to hear to something that was rolling off the tongues of Gary Vaynerchuk and Richard Branson. Maybe it had something to do with those first twenty-four pages of Harari's bestselling book. Whatever the reason, suddenly everything was all about storytelling! Companies were thinking about storytelling. Social media was all about stories. Story was a *thing*.

Facebook posts were stories.

Mission statements were stories.

Websites had entire tabs dedicated to "Our Story."

Taglines were stories.

In some cases, simply saying the word *story* constituted a story. And no one challenged it, because it's all about story.

I won't soon forget the day I walked into a Walgreens in 2018 with my two kids. My seven-year-old son had one too many encounters with the monkey bars on the playground, and his hands were a mess of blisters in varying degrees of popped-ness. Gross.

With swim team practice an hour away, we were in desperate need of waterproof bandages. We were on a mission, but that mission was immediately thwarted when my son insisted he needed to use the facilities. As I stood outside the bathroom door, something caught my eye.

It was an endcap. I'm not even sure what the product was; I could only see one panel from where I was standing, guarding the men's room door. But the bold words "Our Story" jumped off the packaging. Curious, I abandoned my post, walked three steps to the endcap, and picked up a box to read the story I was promised:

> hydraSense® transforms the pure, refreshing power of seawater into gentle comforting hydration. Every drop of seawater in our hydraSense products comes from the Bay of Saint-Malo, France, where powerful tides and currents constantly renew the seawater, creating a wealth of naturally occurring minerals. We then take this mineral-rich seawater, purify and desalinate it to isotonic levels for optimal nasal comfort.[6]

What? *That* is a story?!

I don't think so.

Let's pause here for a second. You've heard an actual story before, right? Someone read you stories at bedtime. Your friends got together for happy hour and exchanged stories. Every holiday crazy Uncle Tom tells the same fishing story. Your spouse went on a business trip and called to tell you about a particularly harrowing incident at a TSA checkpoint. Right?

You've heard a story.

Let me ask you, did the copy on the hydraSense product in any way resemble the stories you hear in your life?

No!

People don't talk like that. And on the occasions they do talk like that, they certainly wouldn't characterize it as a story. Your friends wouldn't say, "I have a story for you" and then recite the items on their grocery list. (If they do, get new friends.)

Herein lies the problem.

In its rise to acceptance, popularity, and buzzword status, we've lost track of what a good story is.

Don't get me wrong. I love that storytelling has become a buzzword in business. I love that people are at least aware there is a place for story in marketing, sales, and leadership. It's a wonderful thing that few seem to disagree with the premise of strategic storytelling. But there is a downside.

In the drastic swing of the storytelling pendulum, we've gone too far. Now we think everything is a story. If you click on the link that says "Our Story," there's no telling what you'll find. Now, when someone says, "This is our story," what follows could be dates, résumé bullet points, ingredients, or who knows what else. I've seen salespeople stand in front of a room and say, "Let me tell you the XYZ company story," and then proceed to flash dates, statistics, and an infographic or two onto a projection screen. I want to stand up and object, just like the professor did in my thesis defense meeting.

Yes. Stories are extremely powerful.

Yes. You should be telling stories to do business. And sometimes we do tell stories to do business.

But stories, somewhere along the way, became known as brands. And somehow we forgot that, no, not everything is a story.

When you look at the advertising, meetings, pitches, and boardrooms of the world, you quickly realize one thing: despite the acceptance of the concept, there's still a lack of actual storytelling in business.

And then, every once in a while, a real story is told, and we remember it.

When a Story Really Is Told

In 2017, I needed a new pair of glasses.

I'd heard of Warby Parker. It seemed like what all the cool kids were doing, so I thought I'd give them a try. Ten days after my appointment and choosing my frames, the glasses arrived at my home.

I opened the box, opened the case, and there they were: a beautiful new set of frames and a little Warby Parker-branded hanky to help keep the lenses clean. The hanky wasn't branded with the Warby Parker logo but rather their story. A real story:

Warby Parker in 100 Words

Once upon a time, a young man left his glasses on an airplane. He tried to buy new glasses. But new glasses were expensive. "Why is it so hard to buy stylish glasses without spending a fortune on them?" he wondered. He returned to school and told his friends. "We should start a company to sell amazing glasses for non-insane prices," said one. "We should make shopping for glasses fun," said another. "We should distribute a pair of glasses to someone in need for every pair sold," said a third. Eureka! Warby Parker was born.[7]

There it was. An actual, rare story.

Just like the biggest Super Bowl commercial of 2014.

It's Not About the Puppies

Spoiler alert: Neither Anheuser-Busch nor Keith Quesenberry needed to worry about their bets. Bud scored big with "Puppy Love." In fact, the ad was rated as the most popular ad not just that year but in the history of the Super Bowl.[8] Better still, it was the most shared ad of the game, with consumers spreading the word about it more than the rest of the top ten combined.[9]

But why? That was what Quesenberry and his colleague Michael Coolsen of Shippensburg University were curious about. To find out and to make their bet on "Puppy Love," they analyzed two years of Super Bowl ads. What they discovered was what made the difference between the top of the polls and the bottom was whether an ad told an actual story. Story beat out sex appeal, humor, celebrity power, and even cute puppies. Quesenberry observed, "It doesn't hurt that the marketer is using a cute puppy, but 60 seconds of a puppy playing with a Budweiser bottle would not have been a hit."[10]

Quesenberry seems to be on to something. If you compare top ten and bottom ten lists, both ends of the ad spectrum take runs at the things you might think would engage viewers: cute characters, great music, humor, and high production value. But only the great stories make the cut.

And therein lies the big question. What the heck *is* a great story?

What It Takes to Tell an Actual Story

Philosophers, writers, readers, and critics have argued about this over the years. For Quesenberry, great story is characterized by something called a five-act structure, which was popularized by Shakespeare. There are seven-act models, nine-point hero's journeys, and w-plots. There are things like prologues and rising action and denouement. There is a never-ending supply of story theory, each more complicated than the other. And this is all fine if your objective is *Hamlet*.

But I'm going out on a limb here and guessing that you, like me, are not trying to write a new Shakespearean masterpiece. I suspect you are more concerned with getting a company off the ground or a product into someone's hands than creating a saga for the ages. You barely have time to proofread your emails, much less conjure a complicated hero's journey.

If that is the case, you're in luck. Great storytelling isn't as complicated as you might think. If what you're trying to do is close some gaps to make your business better, you need a simpler model. No Shakespeare required. You need something you can use at a networking event or toss in a social media post or implement at your next team meeting. You may not be Budweiser or Spielberg or Hemingway or Shakespeare, and you don't want to be. You don't have $4 million to spend, but the stakes are just as high.

What you need are the four essential ingredients that make a story a story.

And a simple way to put them together.

And you have come to the right place.

40

The Four Components of a Great Story

In 2018, my team at the Steller Collective, a firm dedicated to the study, creation, and education of strategic storytelling, decided to put our understanding and story methodology to the test. We wanted to know, without a doubt, what was needed to tell an effective story. What made the difference between a message like the one Warby Parker prints on their lens cloths and the weird one that hydraSense prints on their packaging?

We created a survey designed to test the effectiveness of different types of brand messaging. The hypothesis was this: messages that include certain story components would be more compelling than messages that lacked these components. The components we tested were the ones I'd been inserting into wannabe-story messages for decades:

- Identifiable characters
- Authentic emotion
- A significant moment
- Specific details

Let's break each of these down a little more to ensure we understand them, because once we master these four components, we'll be well on our way to the story promised land.

Identifiable Characters

If you've read any storytelling books before, you've probably read the term "hero." If this is your first storytelling book, you've likely seen motivational messages on Instagram telling you to "be the hero of your own story." And, yes, while the idea of a hero is a classic one, when it comes to telling stories in business, I find this term to be extreme, intimidating, and a little confusing. The word *hero* suggests you need to have done something epic (or at least be dressed in a fancy costume and have wavy locks) in order to have a story to tell. This couldn't be further from the truth.

What every story needs is much simpler than that.

We don't need a hero. We need an identifiable character. Someone we care about and connect to.

To be clear, a character is not a company name. It is not a value someone is committed to. It is not even a large mass of people or even a small group of people. A story needs a single or several single, separate characters we can identify with and connect to.

In "Puppy Love," there are plenty of them, animal and human. Puppies are easy to care about. A man who cares about a puppy? Yes, we are completely okay with that character. An enormous, powerful horse who befriends a tiny puppy? Yep.

Your software? No.

Your soap? No.

Your widget, service, or doodad? Nope.

Unless you turn those things into characters, like M&M's, they're just products. We need a character. Not a hero. An identifiable character.

Authentic Emotion

Another component we believed was essential was the presence of authentic emotion. A list of events or occurrences does not a great story make. A static time line is not a story. The emotion doesn't have to be overly dramatic; it can be as simple or common as frustration or wonder or curiosity. But it needs to be there.

Additionally, and for clarification, emotion does not refer to what the story receiver experiences, but rather the emotion felt by the characters or inherent in the circumstances of the story. It is through that emotion that the story receiver experiences empathy with the story. No emotion means no empathy; no empathy means reduced impact of the message.

Or so we hypothesized.

A Significant Moment

The third component to an effective story is a moment. A specific point in space, time, or circumstance that sets the story aside from the rest of our existence. It's a way to take what might otherwise be a broad, generic description and zoom in tight to allow an audience a better view.

Put another way, remember actual maps? If there was a big city with lots going on, the map often included a few insets, that is, magnified portions of an otherwise sprawling space. That is what a moment does for a story. It homes in on a particular piece of an otherwise sprawling experience or insight. Instead of going big and broad, we need to go small and detailed.

For example, I was recently working with the executives of a private school in New York City who were trying to differentiate themselves in the most competitive educational environment known to man. (My kids go to school in New York City. I have hives just writing this.) They wanted to create a message around the opening of a new international branch of their school in South America. As we got started, their would-be stories included phrases like "It was just so amazing to see the kids experience a different culture . . ." "It was like nothing I'd ever seen . . ." And then they stopped. That was the story, basically the whole map. And because there was no zoomed-in, magnified moment, it was all forgettable.

To fix this, we shifted their language and clarified some moments. Instead of speaking in general terms, they each focused on one incident they had witnessed of a student immersed in a new culture. For one executive, it was during lunch in the cafeteria. The executive expanded on the moment and described watching the kids try new foods and laugh together when the spice of a particular sauce proved too spicy for one of the visiting kids. For another, it was watching the American students negotiate play on the playground. For another, it was walking through the doors of the school on that first Monday morning and noticing how uniquely different the lobby smelled. Zooming in on the act of walking through the doors was what set the moment apart from just a general discussion of being at the school. Each of those moments served to narrow the focus. From there, they could expand on the experience in a general sense, but the clarity of the moment was critical to the effectiveness of the story.

Often, where messages that are intended to be stories go wrong is they stay too vague, too high level, too broad, too general. For a story to be compelling, it should include a specific moment in time or physical space. This component, along with the fourth component, which we'll discuss next, aids in what I call the co-creative process. Where the listeners actively engage in creating a version of the story in their own minds, and in doing so, the story sticks longer.

Specific Details

The specific details component involves the use of specific, descriptive, sometimes unexpected details and imagery that are relevant to the intended audience in an effort to create and draw the listeners into a world that sounds familiar to their own. The finer the detail, the better.

The strongest, stickiest stories are those that master this final component. Using specific details in a story is a way to illustrate how well the teller knows the audience. If, for example, you're telling a story to a 1980s audience, a detail could be a boombox. If you're telling a story to an audience made up of a lot of parents, a detail could be wrestling a stroller into the trunk of a car. Each use of a detail signals to the audience how deeply the teller understands them and builds a strong connection between the audience and the teller and the message.

A recent NPR podcast showcased the work and legacy of marketing genius Tom Burrell. In 1971, Burrell founded one of the first all-black ad agencies and changed the way the world thought about advertising with his slogan: Black people are not dark-skinned white people.[11]

It wasn't uncommon in those days to film two versions of a commercial, one for a white audience and one for a black audience. But instead of developing a unique script for each one, they would write just one script and then film a white version with white actors for the white audience and a black version with black actors for the black audience, completely ignoring the cultural nuances that didn't translate or resonate from one to the other. The commercials always missed the mark.

Burrell pioneered work in advertising that rewrote scripts to make them familiar, relevant, and believable to African American viewers. The Marlboro man wasn't a cowboy out on the open range, but rather a black man in a sweater in an urban city center, and the ad garnered a huge response. Burrell's work was groundbreaking and a perfect example of the importance of using specific details as a way to connect with intended audiences by creating scenes and scenarios familiar to them.

Specific details engage the imagination of the audience. This component pulls the audience deeper into the world of the story, a world that, if done right, will look and feel familiar.

Execution of this final component is a sign of a masterful storyteller. For example, Michelle Obama can thank the specific details component for her speech of a lifetime at the 2016 Democratic National Convention. All politics aside, what made the now former first lady's speech so powerful was the use of story and, most importantly, her masterful use of the specific details component to draw Americans in and drive her message deep into their psyche.

The story started strong when, at the 1:16 mark, the former first lady used the moment component to take her audience to a very specific point in time: "A journey that started soon after we arrived in Washington. When they set off for their first day at their new school. I will never forget that winter morning."

She then included a few specific details of her daughters departing for their first day: "I saw their little faces pressed up against the window."

And there it was. Sending your kid to school for the first time is a moment filled with emotion, a moment likely burned into your memory if you're a parent. Whether you put them on a bus or drove them there yourself, you likely watched your children's "little faces" and saw your life flash before your eyes.

Don't have kids? No worries. You no doubt remember the first time you set off for something new and can match the emotion. In either case, by choosing a detail many people in her audience could relate to, Michelle Obama put everyone on the same page and in the same emotional place. With those few familiar details, she commanded the room and the country.

Putting Story to the Test

Once our team had these four components in place, we meticulously administered a national online survey of 1,648 respondents administered by Edison Research. Respondents, all of whom were parents, were presented with two messages: a generic control message about a children's toy product called Builder.co and a randomly selected version of a message about the same children's toy that included either one, two, three, or all four of the components listed above. Additionally, the order in which the two messages, generic or storied, were presented was rotated in order to counteract recency and latency bias.

After reading each one, respondents rated how compelling they found the messages. Respondents were then asked to choose which of the two messages they found more compelling, more entertaining, more memorable, more persuasive, and more captivating.

I must admit, when the survey was released into the world, I felt a sense of unease and flashed back to my thesis defense. Would our hypothesis be supported? Is this really what makes a great story?

I will also admit to some celebration when the results came back with an overwhelming "yes." In all cases, even if the message contained just one of the components, it performed better than the message with none of the components. Additionally, the more components the message contained, the more appealing the story became. Sixty-three percent of the respondents who received both messages said the story with all four components was more compelling, entertaining, memorable, persuasive, and captivating than the message with none, which, incidentally, was a message that sounded a lot like the brand messages we've gotten used to hearing.

These results should be particularly exciting to you. I mean, yes, if you happen to know Jake Scott, have $4 million, and can get access to the best ad agencies, dog trainers, and horse whisperers in the business, maybe these findings don't matter much to you. You can probably just pay other people to understand story for you.

But what if you don't have those things? How do you create a message worthy of the Super Bowl?

Well, now you know. The reason the Budweiser ad fared so well, according to experts and explained by our research, had more to do with story than anything else. And story costs nothing. It simply requires a few key components.

What you have now is a simple checklist of what your story needs. You don't need millions of dollars. You don't need outrageous conflict or some complicated journey (the Builder.co story was about a dad who wished he could spend better quality time with his kids). All you need is a character, some emotion, a moment, and a detail or two to create a sense of familiarity, and 63 percent of people will find your message more compelling than if you didn't.

Now that you know the essential and tested components of what makes a great story, all that's left is to put those components together somehow. I've got you covered there as well, and per the usual, I'll keep it simple.

The Steller Storytelling Framework

"A story has a beginning, a middle, and an end." I can still hear Mrs. Carlson, my third-grade teacher, saying from the front of the room. She was giving us one of the earliest writing assignments I can remember. I later wrote something about a zebra, and allegedly that notebook still exists somewhere. Who could have guessed that my third-grade composition lesson would still be with me today? And Mrs. Carlson was not wrong. Beginning, middle, and end are the building blocks of any story, and business stories are no different. But there *is* a more descriptive way of approaching these three literary acts. After all, we're not in third grade anymore. From now on, let's try thinking of them as *normal, explosion,* and *new normal.*

The first time I heard a story described this way was at a storytelling retreat with my favorite storyteller, Donald Davis. When he laid this groundwork, or something very similar, I felt as if all of the stories I had ever lived or told made sense. He put words to what my storytelling heart had always known but never knew how to say. It may sound cheesy, like an over-the-top storytelling love story, but it's true. That simple framework influenced every story I told before or worked on since, and I hope it will do the same for you.

Let's take a closer look at each of these three story pieces that make up the Steller storytelling framework.

Normal

A bad story has a single defining characteristic: we don't care. Even the flashiest of colors, the biggest of budgets, or the cutest of puppies can't make us care. They might get our attention, but they can't make us invest emotionally. They can't influence and transform. Fortunately, the majority of the time, the root cause of this disconnect can be traced back to a single mistake: leaving out the first part of the story. The normal.

For example, this is why we can watch the local five o'clock news every night without bawling our eyes out. The news usually starts in the middle of the story—the robbery, the fire, the car accident. Although each of these instances is worthy of tears, the broadcasters don't have the time to tell us anything about the people (the identifiable characters). We don't know who the people are. We don't know what emotions they were thinking about or hoped for or felt before tragedy struck. We don't know anything about them, and so we don't care.

To tell a good story, one your audience will care about and invest in, you have to start off strategically by establishing the normal. The way things were before something changed. The normal is where you take a little bit of time to include the key components of a story: introduce the identifiable characters and their emotions. This is also where you include a few details that create a sense of familiarity for the audience, drawing them in. They let down their guards. They put themselves in the characters' shoes.

Done right, throughout the process of the normal, the audience is saying to themselves, "I recognize that person. Yes, I understand what this is about. Yes, I can see how they would feel that way." The guy on the plane who left his glasses. A couple falling in love. A young, future American president with charm who had to have that amazing French cologne. We'll talk more about the normal throughout the next section of the book, but for now know that this is the most important part of the story. The normal is where you include the components. The normal is where you give your audience a reason to care. The normal is the part most people leave out, which is why their stories don't stick.

Explosion

Admittedly, the word *explosion* is a little aggressive. It implies blood or injury or fire. That is not necessarily the case in your story, though. The explosion, for our purposes, is simply the happening. It could be a big thing or a small thing, a good thing or a bad thing. Most importantly, it's the moment things change. Perhaps it is a realization or a decision. It may be an actual event. Whatever the case, the explosion is the point in the story where things were going along as normal and then suddenly they are different. Good different, bad different, doesn't matter.

For now, remember:

Normal: Things are how they are.
Explosion: Something happens.
New Normal: Things are different.

New Normal

The third and final phase is the new normal. This is where you share with your audience what life is like now, after the explosion. You tell them what you know now, why you are wiser or stronger or how you improved (or are still trying to improve) as a result. It could be a moral. It could be when a client lived happily ever after, after using your product or service. It could include a call to action. However it comes together, the new normal is why storytelling works as a strategy to convey a point or enhance a message and not just to entertain. The new normal is what makes a story worth listening to in business.

Just the Beginning . . .

So cute puppies and talented directors don't guarantee great stories. Despite what some may tell you, a mission statement isn't a story. A brand isn't a story. Marketing jargon isn't a story. Additionally, a story doesn't have to be complicated. Introduce a few characters, paint a picture using a particular moment in time with specific details and the emotions involved, and you're on your way to story success.

The next question, of course, is, which stories should you use? There are an infinite number of them. Where do you even start?

There are four key story types that appear over and over again in business. They are the stories that illustrate not only what you offer but why and how. No matter what the gap is in your business, one of these four stories will be the bridge you need.

Sometimes the best way to learn to tell a great story is to see others at work. Each of the following four essential stories has its characters and its audience. Each has a purpose in your business. You don't need to create all of them at once. But when it comes to the infinite universe of possible tales, understanding these four types of business stories will help you decide not only which ones to tell but how best to tell them.

That's what we'll tackle next.

PART TWO

The Four Essential Stories

The Tales Every Business Needs to Tell

CHAPTER FOUR

The Value Story

How Storytelling Drives
Sales and Marketing

Marketing is no longer about the stuff that you make,
but about the stories you tell.
— SETH GODIN, AUTHOR AND ENTREPRENEUR

The Workiva sales team had an advantage over the competition. The kind of advantage that meant there really was no competition.

The solution they offered their customers was unmatched: it was the best in accuracy and simplicity, and it enabled efficiencies that shaved hours, even days, off of processes that tied up even the best and brightest

Fortune 100 companies. Essentially, Workiva spared companies embarrassment from high-profile errors, saved companies millions of dollars, and offered solutions that changed people's lives.

So you would think that saying yes to Workiva would be a no-brainer. Like, duh.

And yet Workiva struggled as much as the next guy to build a bridge strong enough to get potential clients to say yes. Not because Workiva couldn't deliver. They absolutely could, and their long list of converts and impeccable customer satisfaction score were proof. But even after the sales team pitched decision makers, even after they demonstrated every possible life-changing feature, there was still so often an elephant in the room.

The reluctance toward change.

Turns out Workiva's biggest competition wasn't another company or product; it was the status quo. Sure, their platform might be more effective and efficient, but they couldn't overcome basic human nature—the nature that says the devil you know is better than the savior you don't.

Burdened with the undeniable sense that the way they were currently communicating their value wasn't enough, they were determined to figure out a better way. Workiva's plan? To switch their focus from features and benefits to stories.

Instead of using more data to support their claims—they were already giving more data than even the savviest data maniac could handle—they would tell stories that tapped into the real pain of the current problems. They would tell stories that highlighted the real-life implications of inefficiency and inaccuracy. They had these stories; they just weren't deliberate in telling them. All of that was about to change.

I had the honor of working with the exceptional team at Workiva to help bring their true value to life through stories, and the stories they found were as remarkable as the product they sold.

One story was designed to illustrate the value of a particular feature of their product that guaranteed data consistency in critical documents, something that, prior to Workiva, was only possible via endless hours of manual checking and rechecking. The accountants hated the process because it sucked the life out of them and basically meant they had to sacrifice all nonwork passions and commitments. The companies hated it because they had no choice but to pay for hours and hours and hours of backtracking and double-checking that really should have only taken a fraction of the time and cost a fraction of the payroll.

Again, the Workiva solution seemed like a no-brainer. And yet logic wasn't getting the job done. So, instead, they learned to tell a story. It was the story of an investor relations customer who, not willing to let middle-age damn him to a dad bod for eternity, decided to focus on fitness. And not just any fitness. Being a goal-driven man, he set his eyes on a triathlon.

Ah, the triathlon. So much more than its cousin, the marathon, which involves merely running, the triathlon is the ultimate test of fitness. Swimming, biking, running. All three components require their own preparation, equipment, and planning, which means deciding to do a triathlon instantly signs you up for a massive commitment. And not just a physical commitment, but a massive time commitment. It's basically a second job. And while the pay isn't great, the benefits (and bragging rights) can be amazing.

The investor relations executive knew this, and he wasn't afraid. He bought a killer road bike, a pair of elite running shoes, and a membership at a fancy gym with an Olympic-sized pool. He was as methodical about his training as he was about his work in data reporting. He used a spreadsheet to keep track of pool times and the miles he ran and biked. He had it all planned out. He would hit the gym for swims before work and then run or bike after he left the office.

But then came the quarterly close, and this executive was responsible for getting financials from one team and incorporating them into his slide decks and reports. Each quarter he would meet with the other reporting team. They would sit in a conference room and meticulously update the numbers to make sure, without a doubt, that the data he was using was accurate to the very last minute.

Of course, because everyone's days were already filled with all the other work they were supposed to be doing, these extra financial accuracy meetings either had to happen before business hours (there goes swimming time) or after office hours (bye-bye run time). Despite his best efforts and flawless training spreadsheets, the man found himself forced to leave the bike on the rack and the speedo in the car and, instead of training, head to a fluorescent-lit conference room to meet, again, with the financial reporting team.

Sadly, with so many training sessions skipped and not enough time to make up the difference, the man had to withdraw from the triathlon he was so excited to compete in. Heartbroken and frustrated, the man wondered if he'd ever have enough time to do what it took to achieve his goal.

Everything changed the day that man's company started using Workiva's platform. Now, his reports and slides were connected to the reporting team's, which meant anytime a number changed, his reports were updated automatically. No more double- and triple-checking. No more before-hours or after-hours meetings. Most importantly, no more stressing about data consistency, because the numbers were always right. It was all done for him and done more accurately than if they had done it themselves.

Not only did the company get better reporting as a result, they also increased employee satisfaction. After all, what employee likes wasting time on inefficiencies? The reporting team didn't have to waste time rehashing numbers, and most importantly, now the executive could spend his precious pre- and post-office time swimming and biking and running to his disappearing dad-bod's content.

Two quarters later, the executive completed his first triathlon—with the folks from the reporting team there to cheer him on.

Equipped with this story, what used to be a bullet point in Workiva's demo presentation could now be an emotional moment in the value journey. What previously might have been glossed over, either by the Workiva team presenting it or the potential clients who, heaven forbid, had slightly tuned out as people in meetings tend to do, was now being heard in one engaging, entertaining, and (significantly) relevant moment that perfectly demonstrated how valuable a solution like this is, not only to the bottom line, not only to fiduciary responsibilities, but to the people who make an organization run.

The Value Story

This is the first gap in business: the value gap.

The gap between the problem and the value of the solution.

The gap between the product and the value to the customer.

The most important gap any business needs to bridge is the gap between what they offer and the people who, whether they know it or not, need it. To capture the attention of buyers, to convince them that, yes, this is the solution, and eventually to transform them into repeat users, customers, buyers, believers. When it comes to sales and marketing, the *value story* is king. And the value of a value story starts in psychology and spans the full spectrum of why we say yes.

The Information Temptation

The challenge Workiva faced—the challenge we all face—was to resist the temptation to try to close the gaps with things like features and functions or capabilities and advanced technologies. No one is immune from the temptation to complicate the journey across the value gap. Not even the local gelato shop.

When my family recently took a beach vacation, as most beach vacations require, we stopped at a gelato shop on our walk home after dinner. We'd been there many times before, and it was always packed with a line out the door and spilling into the street. But what was typically jolly summer vacation chaos had a subtly different tone on this particular trip. People seemed agitated, impatient, and there were noticeably more parents speaking in terse tones to their children. When it was finally our turn at the counter, I understood why.

Instead of the rows of colorful frozen treats on display with slices of corresponding fruits or chocolate candies to signify the flavor you would typically expect from a gelato shop, there were two rows of round metal lids sitting atop what one could only hope were buckets of gelato. Gone was the luxury of picking the brown one or the pink one or the pale green one with crumbled pistachios on it; instead, you now had to read the flavors from a list posted on the wall behind the gelato-scooping staff.

Scan a variety of pretty colors and fruits and choose the flavor that looks most delicious: easy.

Read flavors from a list, mentally compare each option, logically assess which one might taste best: hard.

Add in the additional challenge of having to read off the flavors to kids who can't read and then repeat those flavors because what child can process fifteen different flavors in a list, and the struggle was real. In just five minutes in the shop I heard three sets of agitated parents threaten their children that if they didn't decide, they didn't get anything at all. (I may or may not have been one of them.)

While more information may seem like the way to make an obvious decision more obvious, the reality is this approach often muddies up an otherwise easy yes. And while more data or details or logical explanations are often what the audience expects you to say, if your goal is to convince them of the value you're offering, the facts may do more harm than good. Why? Because they simply make our brains work harder than they need to or, for that matter, want to.

One Brain, Two Systems

In his *New York Times* bestselling book *Thinking, Fast and Slow*, 2002 winner of the Nobel Prize in economics Daniel Kahneman discusses in great detail what he refers to as the two systems of the brain: System 1 and System 2.

System 1 "operates automatically and quickly with little or no effort and no sense of voluntary control."[1] System 1 is responsible for automatic answers to questions like, "What is 2 + 2?" This first system is the reason we know to look to the sky when we hear thunder or a passing jet and not the ground. Based on a lifetime of cues, System 1 allows us to take in information, assimilate it, and make judgments on it simultaneously and effortlessly. Do we get it wrong sometimes? Sure. For example, how many of each animal did Moses bring on the ark? System 1 says two. Of course, that's incorrect. Moses was more into burning bushes; Noah was the ark guy.

That's where System 2 comes in. System 2 "allocates attention to the effortful mental activities that demand it, including complex computations. The operations of System 2 are often associated with the subjective experience of agency, choice, and concentration."[2] Whew. If you're as tired as I was just reading that, it means your System 2 was at work. System 2 requires concentration and effort. System 2 processes new information. System 2 gets involved once System 1 determines the issue at hand is too complicated.

Simply put, System 1 is characterized by *cognitive ease* while System 2 involves *cognitive strain*.

Read that statement again. Cognitive ease versus cognitive strain.

If, such as in the case of Workiva, the value of what you have to offer is relatively obvious, if you believe (which I'm sure you do) that your product or service will make a positive difference in the lives of your customers and the decision should be easy, then why would you ever want to engage System 2 and cause cognitive strain?!

A System 2 approach can ruin an otherwise great experience, as I learned that fateful day in the gelato shop. The only redeeming feature of the cruel System-2 hijacking that day was that I had just finished reading the cognitive ease section of Kahneman's book and knew immediately what was happening. I experienced firsthand how important it is that brands, companies, and businesspeople in general keep their customers in the System 1 space. When it comes to creating persuasive messages, Kahneman said, "The general principle is that anything you can do to reduce cognitive strain will help."[3] While your message may be true, if it isn't easy enough for your audience to believe it and accept it as truth with System 1, they will call in System 2. And when System 2 is involved, the likelihood of cognitive strain, followed by frustration and agitation, greatly increases.

Lists are bait for System 2.

Bullet points are bait for System 2.

Price comparisons are bait for System 2.

Features are bait for System 2.

Benefits are bait for System 2.

Of course, in the case of the gelato shop, it wasn't a matter of value story versus no value story. But, whether you're in the business of sweet treats, used cars, luxury real estate, or medical sales, when it comes to communicating the value of what you offer, you have a choice. Logic or common sense. Strain or ease. Information or story.

The value story gives System 1 the ability to do what it does best: go with the flow, accept the story as it's told, and not bother System 2, which tends to make people tired and cranky. Story is the System 1 love language, and the value story is the perfect bridge to get your customers and stakeholders from facts to feelings. Not only that, marketing researcher Jennifer Edson Escala of Vanderbilt University found that audiences responded more positively and accepted ideas more readily when they come in story form.[4] Beyond simply being engaging, stories actually prime the brain to be more open to what you're offering.

For example, have you ever been on a flight that ends with a pitch for a credit card? I'm on a lot of flights, and without fail, about forty minutes before landing, the flight attendant makes a special announcement for "this flight only." Surprise, it's their exclusive credit card they pitch on every flight. The attendant lists interest rates and annual fees and baggage allowances and how many miles you get (usually sixty thousand, which is enough for blah blah blah). On a recent flight from Dallas to Orlando, I looked around the cabin during the credit card commercial, and no one even looked up, much less listened.

When the attendant finishes the announcement, I am often tempted to stand up and ask for the mic. I'd signed up for one of those cards before, and what I got in return was so much more than extra baggage allowance.

I would tell my fellow passengers the story of the European trip I was able to take with my husband and how the miles from the card allowed me to upgrade our trip from coach to business class as a surprise. I will never forget the moment we stepped on the plane and the flight attendant showed my husband to his seat—a fully reclining pod. Michael looked at me in disbelief and excitement. We'd never flown in such luxury before, and the joy I felt being able to give him that surprise was priceless. That card and those extra miles gave us a memory I will cherish and made an unforgettable vacation even better.

I can't help but wonder if more people would be open to what the airline was offering, more primed to say yes, and would sign up if they heard that story, or *any* story for that matter. My educated guess is yes. If it were a story, people would look up. If it had characters, emotions, and details, people would envision themselves and their loved ones in the same situation. If there was a specific moment, like stepping onto the plane, people would engage in the co-creative process. And if those components were all arranged in a normal–explosion–new normal format, by the time the story came to a close, the passengers would all be ringing their flight-attendant call buttons, unable to resist what the attendants were selling.

"It's So Much More than That . . ."

When a sale doesn't close or a marketing message doesn't convert, there is a sense that the true value of the product was missed. That it's worth so much more than the message conveyed. The value of a weight-loss program is so much more than the food you're supposed to buy or the trainer you're supposed to hire. The value of a weight-loss program is measured in renewed confidence, in rekindling depleted passion, in energy to do what you love.

The value of an advanced telemedical device is so much more than the cost of the equipment. The value of an advanced telemedical device is measured in the joy, relief, and spared sorrow of a family whose child had a medical emergency in a remote part of the world and survived because top-level physicians could be virtually at the scene.

The value of a cloud-based technology solution is so much more than the monthly subscription fee. The value isn't limited to the hours the technology can save. The value of a cloud-based technology system, like what Workiva offers, is also measured in what the people do with the hours they save: compete in triathlons, attend kids' T-ball games, fulfill dreams.

If you represent or have created a product, service, or company, and you have a passion for spreading the word about this superior product to the world, you've probably said, or at least thought, those very words: "Yes, this is a [insert name of product/service here] and it does X, Y, Z, but it's so much more than that." The challenge is, what typically follows is more words, information, and attempts to justify when what this situation really calls for is a value story to illustrate the value and usefulness.

Perhaps one of the greatest executions of this "so much more" exercise was by Apple during the 2014 holiday season with their commercial titled "Misunderstood."

The commercial opens with soft holiday music playing while a family piles into a car on a dreary winter day. They pull onto a snow-lined street and make their way to their grandparents' home and are met with the sweet greetings of reunion. It's the quintessential family at Christmas time, including the angsty teenager. The floppy-haired young man can't seem to be bothered with family activities. He's on his iPhone through every event and activity. Grandpa hug? iPhone. Snow angels? iPhone. Baking cookies? iPhone. The teen is seemingly unengaged in anything beyond whatever is happening on his phone.

Until Christmas morning.

The family is packed into the cozy family room, pajama-clad and happily opening presents. The Christmas tree is lit, and the room's loud with laughter. The angsty, floppy-haired teen abruptly stands and turns on the television. The room goes quiet in confusion. The teen swipes his iPhone at it, and suddenly the screen is filled with a slideshow of the last few days. Instead of being engrossed in a game or social media on his iPhone, the teen had been documenting all their beautiful family memories as a gift. Scenes of love and happiness flash across the screen. Every snowball thrown, every smile, every little detail has been captured and preserved for the family to enjoy for years to come. His grateful family is full of smiles and happy tears as they watch. When the video concludes, they pull the teen in for a long overdue hug.

A hug that makes me cry every time.

A hug that meant so much more than a list of features ever could.

Apple had a choice, just as we all have a choice. A choice to simply focus on the features of the phone. You can imagine what *that* commercial would look like because they've done it. A pleasant male voice walks you through the intuitive, "all in the palm of your hand" moviemaking possibilities of iPhones. The professional editing capabilities. The exquisite picture quality because of the superior camera technology. The excessive storage, which makes saving these videos possible in the first place. On the screen, we would see the phone rotate on a white background with various jump shots to show the features in action. It would be cool, no doubt, but I doubt it would have a fraction of the impact.

Instead, because Apple chose to tell a story, we get an opportunity to see what the product could actually mean in our lives. That it could bring us together. That it could create moments we cherish.

Of course, not everyone loved this advertisement. And when Apple won the 2014 Emmy for best commercial, people were quick to claim all the ways the ad missed the mark: not enough attention paid to the product features, any smartphone can make a movie, and other comments that showcase exactly what is wrong with marketing today.

As Ken Segall, once the creative director of Steve Jobs's ad agency, so eloquently put it, "There are tens of millions of people who will stop in their tracks at this commercial and wipe a tear from their eye. As a result, they will feel slightly more attached to Apple, which is the marketing purpose of this spot."[5]

Please note these key pieces of that statement: "stop in their tracks," "wipe a tear from their eye," and "feel slightly more attached to Apple." At the time this spot aired, Apple was facing a bit of a backlash (the U2 album debacle). The bridge they needed to build had to be heavy on captivation and transformation elements for it to work. Pushing too hard on influence could have caused further trouble. Wrapping the features in a heartfelt story of a teenager and his family struck the perfect value chord.

Segall concluded, "The reactions have been universally glowing. . . . [The ad] lines up perfectly with the values Apple has communicated for years. It's not about technology—it's about quality of life."[6]

People don't buy the *thing*. They buy what the thing will *do* for them.

In order for them to do that, you have to tell them a story.

That story is a value story.

How to Make the Value Story Shift

As much as I love the "Misunderstood" commercial, it still comes from Apple.

I don't know about you, but as a frequent reader of business books and online magazines, I find the incessant Apple examples a bit nauseating. Yes, Apple, one of the biggest companies in the world, got it right. But what if you aren't Apple? What if you don't have unlimited resources and the most brilliant ad agencies falling over themselves to create a value message for you? How do you do it? How do you shift from focusing on features to telling the story of the problems those features solve?

Fair question, and one Chelsea Scholz had to answer, because she wasn't given any other choice.

In 2016, Chelsea faced a double dilemma in her role as a campaign strategist at Unbounce, a web-based operation offering a set of tools to help digital marketers increase website and campaign conversions. In plain English, Unbounce helps you do a better job of getting people to take action when they visit your website, such as subscribe by email, make a purchase, or try a product. When someone takes action, they've converted from an online, virtual window shopper to someone engaged with your business in some real, tangible way.

Conversion is a big deal. Unlike a Super Bowl ad, where conversion is notoriously difficult to track, conversion on a website is famously and satisfyingly measurable. As controversial as it may seem, most people visiting a website are dragging a host of information along with them, namely, a pile of data ranging from their demographics and technology use to their shopping habits and book preferences.

That data is essentially oxygen for internet marketers. Every visitor is tracked, every action recorded, every sale traced back to its source. There is perhaps no more quantifiable marketing than online marketing.

That same strength, however, can develop into an Achilles' heel. Over time, it has led many online businesses to become obsessive about data and forget there are real humans behind it. That was the first of Chelsea's two dilemmas. She said, "At Unbounce we'd been heavily data-driven for the past eighteen months. Everything we produced was driven by KPIs [key performance indicators] and objectives, and it felt like we were wandering into a realm of talking at people instead of *to* people."

This dilemma wasn't Unbounce's alone. It's one that has permeated the marketing world as a whole, a dilemma I inadvertently stumbled upon in September 2015—the first time I spoke at a digital marketing conference.

Roughly 350 of the brightest minds in online advertising, content marketing, and search engine optimization had gathered for a two-day, one-track conference packed with highly technical keynotes about, I mean, I can't even really tell you, it was *that* technical. I remember presenters talking about personas and retargeting and—. I was lost after that. I was so lost, in fact, I went back to my room and considered telling the event organizers I had a family emergency and wouldn't be able to present. The desire to flee became more intense when, as an "end of the first day" closer, the event had all the presenters take the stage to give one piece of digital advice. We stood in a line on the stage, and when it was my turn, I mumbled something about people and stories. The room fell silent and 350 sets of eyes stared at me and then at each other. They all seemed to ask, What is she even saying?

I would love to say the awkwardness was imagined—and honestly that's what I was hoping—but, alas, it was real and confirmed by several well-meaning attendees at the social hour at the end of the first day. "Oh . . . I'm sure you'll be fine" they comforted me over Hawaiian-BBQ-themed sliders.

The next morning I decided to face my fears and speak. Besides, I figured, judging by how much everyone was drinking the night before, they likely won't show up for the opening keynote, who, of course, was me.

I was wrong.

When 9:00 a.m. rolled around, the room was packed. After all, they had paid a hefty price to attend. Or maybe, like passing a wreck on the freeway, they wanted to see for themselves what my inevitable crash and burn would look like. Either way, I had a job to do. So I told the digital marketers a story and then taught them about the art of storytelling. To my surprise—and everyone else's, according to tweets like "Who would have thought the storyteller would be the best keynote of the event?!" (thanks, man)—it was a session worth attending.

Of course, I would like to take credit, to believe it was my particular oratorical skills that hit the mark, but I know something much bigger was at play. These were brilliant people who were very good at what they did. But as the data increases and the metrics become more trackable, it's easy to get sucked into the analytics of it all and, in the process, forget that, on the other side of those metrics, is a person.

A person with a problem.

A person who needs you to solve that problem.

A person who needs a story to captivate them, assure them your solution is the right one, and turn them into a believer.

That September 2015 event was the first of what became many digital marketing presentations for me. And because, yes, there *is* a place for metrics, I was thrilled to be rated at the top of the speaker roster. Several digital marketing conferences later, and without knowing it at the time, Chelsea from Unbounce and I crossed paths.

Chelsea's concerns about Unbounce's marketing were percolating. This was dilemma number one. And because fate has a sense of humor, Chelsea had been tasked with creating a video to explain to existing customers why they should get excited about a new product called Unbounce Convertables.

Convertables was a tool within Unbounce's preexisting landing-page builder that allowed digital marketers to do a lot of the work of creating and testing conversion tools—such as pop-ups and sticky bars—without needing to ask a programmer to do the work. With almost no technical savvy, in seconds you could tweak your online conversion tools as often as you wanted and measure the results. No geeks required. For anyone trying to grow their own business in the twenty-first century, what they were offering was pure magic.

So, yes, Convertables was a powerful tool with plenty of benefits. But there was one catch: Unbounce didn't yet want to talk about what the product *was*. Until it was launched, the exact details of Convertables were to remain secret. That was dilemma number two.

How on earth could Chelsea get the point across without being able to talk about, well, the point? How could she present a product if she couldn't talk about it?

What Chelsea inadvertently stumbled onto, however, was both a problem and a solution, one that anyone could use.

If you can't talk about your product or show it to anyone, what would you say to customers?

The moment you start to think that way, everything changes.

Forget the Product, What's the Problem?

Ignoring what your business offers can seem like heresy for the uninitiated. But doing so does one critical thing: it forces you to focus on the customer. If you can't talk about your product, what's left? Answer: the people using it.

The people who might use your product are your customers and prospects. And they're humans, not data. And that means they respond to story.

Chelsea discovered this when she began to wrestle with her dilemma. Since she couldn't talk about the product, there was nothing left to talk about but the people. And as she kept her focus on her customers long enough, something emerged: clarity about their problem. After much back-and-forth and little progress, Chelsea finally had a breakthrough.

"It clicked for me," she said. "Talk about the pain they might be having in their own marketing. Tell a freaking story about it. I realized that everything we did needed a story that people could relate to. Otherwise we were just talking to cyborgs and echo chambers."

Chelsea had been backed in a messaging corner that only a value story could get her out of. It shifted the focus to customers at a time when the greatest temptation was to do exactly the opposite. And while it didn't make her job easier (storytelling, while the better choice, is rarely the easiest), being forced into this messaging corner gave her no choice but to approach the message differently and tell a story.

Unbounce's Value Story

The Unbounce "You Are a Marketer" video is simple, effective, and, best of all, it worked.

The story opens with a black-and-white closeup of two expressionless eyes. As the narrator speaks, we pull back to discover the eyes belong to the typical Unbounce customer: a marketing professional in front of his laptop. He remains expressionless, and as the camera slowly pulls back, his problems are revealed: little budget, no technical experience, and more than anything, no power to take control of the marketing process.

In the words of our Steller storytelling framework, that's the normal for this poor guy, and it's where we learn about the pain.

The explosion arrives when he finally blinks, and we hear that Unbounce has a new conversion tool coming. When the marketer opens his eyes, he's in the new normal: the world is in color, not black and white. As we pull back again, he's a changed man, smiling and sipping a cup of coffee.

It was simple, inexpensive, and it worked. Chelsea said, "We centered the video visuals around that person (a.k.a. an identifiable character). It was clean. It was easy, and it not only spread the message and the hype that we were looking for, but actually resulted in lead generation *and* new customers for us. And, like I said, we didn't even say what we were releasing yet!"

The Unbounce story never shows the product. In fact, other than mention that a product was coming, the ad barely even talks about it.

The entire shot is focused on the person who matters (the marketer), the problem the person faces (figuring out what to do when a marketing funnel runs dry), and the happily-ever-after when the problem is solved.

For Unbounce, the story results were even better than they hoped. The video delivered over twelve hundred interested subscribers, more than ten times Chelsea's goal. And, as Unbounce can vouch, email addresses from people who are truly interested in your product are gold. They convert, which is digital marketing speak for *buy*.

But I Love My Statistics

Let's pause for a moment here, because I think it's very important for you to understand just how much I, a lover of stories, live for data. Seriously. If I were to write my dating profile, it would include the following: "Don't care if you love dogs, but must appreciate the tallying of various activities to support the achievement of specific goals." I track the food I eat, the number of quality hours I spend with my family each week, and how many words I write a day. I track how much I weigh, how often I meditate, and a variety of other metrics that are a bit too personal to share here.

So before you allow yourself to think we've gone too deep into the qualitative pool to be quantitatively relevant, let me assure you: the story needs your data, the case needs the proof. System 1 needs System 2, or poor Moses will be stuck building an ark. It's the approach to the information that needs an adjustment.

Remember Mary Poppins? The nanny all other nannies could never measure up to? When the children refused to take their medicine, she paired the healing concoction with a spoonful of sugar. Just as dog parents hide their puppy pills in peanut butter or, as my mom was prone to do, crush up Tylenol tablets and mix them in with applesauce (a food I still regard with a hint of suspicion), so you should wrap your data/logic/points/information in a story.

The formula is really quite simple. Start with a story. Draw them in, captivate them, get buy-in from System 1 so they've already said yes. Then insert the information. Give the facts, appeal to logic, put as much data in there as will make you comfortable. But then come back to the story. Wrap the whole thing up with the new normal. Much like a spoonful of sugar, as long as the message begins and ends with the story, it'll go down nice and easy.

The following is a detailed guide for using the Steller storytelling framework and components to create a perfect value story.

A Breakdown of the Storytelling Framework

If ever the storytelling framework were built for a specific story type, the value story is it. The Steller storytelling framework basically begs for values stories to be told.

Think about it. A customer or prospect has a pain or a problem. They're struggling with it, they're dealing with it, they're trying to figure out a better way. Normal. Then you or your company comes along. The customer engages with your product or solution or service. Explosion. Now, life is better. The pain is cured, the problem is solved, and the customer is so much better off than before. New normal.

In other words:

1. Normal
   - What is your customers' problem?
   - What pain are they experiencing?
   - How do they feel?
   - How is it impacting their life? Their business?
   - What's keeping them awake at night?
2. Explosion
   - How does your product/service solve the pain or problem?
   - How does your product/service make their life easier?
   - What does the experience of using your product/service feel like for the customers?
   - How is using your product/service different?
3. New Normal
   - How is life different after?
   - What is enhanced or improved?
   - How do the customers feel?
   - What pain points have vanished?

With that basic framework as your guide, what makes a value story really strike a chord, hit the mark, or [insert additional clichés here] is the inclusion and execution of the four story components.

The Value Story: A Components Breakdown

As we learned in chapter 3, several essential components make a story not only great but a story in the first place. Don't stress. Incorporating them is super simple and in many cases totally obvious. But in the interest of making sure you never have to question your value stories again, I'll detail for you the nuances of each component when they appear in the value story.

Identifiable Characters

Where most would-be value stories run off the rails is right here. With the identifiable character. And I get it. It's easy to get confused. To think that, if you're trying to get people to understand the value of a product, the product should be the star of the story. The product can do this! *and* that! *and*, oh, did you see how this product is better than that product because of this, this, and . . . wait for it . . . *this?!*

The important thing to remember is that when it comes to great storytelling, and as the research indicates, having an actual character for the audience to connect with and relate to is key.

Having an identifiable character is a critical point of distinction between a strong story and a weak one. The greatest mistake of marketing is to put what you offer at the center of everything instead of the person you offer it *to*. It's focusing on the software, the burger, the makeup, the car, the widget instead of the person who will use the software, eat the burger, wear the makeup, drive the car, or benefit from the widget. Unless you work at Pixar, cars aren't characters. People are characters. Products don't win the girl, overcome the odds, or slay the dragon. People do those things. The knight in shining armor is the character, the sword is the product, the dragon is the problem. Sure, the knight uses the sword. But it's the knight who slays the dragon, not the sword. The sword is just a tool to solve a problem. Take away the knight, and you don't have a story. You just have a piece of metal stuck in a rock.

When you go to craft your value story, make sure it includes a character: a person or, in the case of Budweiser, a lovable animal. Include a few details about the character. It could be something as simple as an age, a personality trait, a physical characteristic, a profession, or a specific thing they wear. One or two small details help build out the image of the character in the minds of the audience, and the more clearly they can imagine the character, the more they will connect with the content.

In the Apple ad, it was easy to understand a distracted teenager.

In the Workiva story, people related to an overworked man with hopes beyond a fluorescent-lit boardroom.

I'll say it again—for a value story to work, it must include a character. Not simply your product. Not your factory, office, technology, code, or widget. Not your logo, brand, pitch, or plan. A value story is nothing without a character to care about.

As for the product? The beautiful part of the value story, like for Chelsea and Unbounce, is that you don't even need to talk about the product. We don't need to really see it or totally understand it. All we need to understand is that the product changed the course of the identifiable character's life and, subsequently, how it could change our own.

Authentic Emotion

I heard a sales guru say that in order to fully connect with the needs of your potential customers, you had to get into bed with them.

Yes. I thought it was creepy too. Which, looking back, I think is exactly what he wanted—to sound a little controversial. That being said, the point he eventually went on to make was, in order to figure out what your customers really care about, imagine them at the end of the day. They finish dinner with their family or maybe they don't get to see their families because they're working too late. Maybe they pay a few bills, wrap up a few emails, watch some late-night television, and then, in those few minutes when the lights are off and they're about ready to fall asleep . . .

What keeps them awake?

What problem are they staring at the ceiling and trying to solve but can't? What issue is worrying them, concerning them, stressing them out? Once you know that, then the next step is how do *you* fix that feeling?

And while I much prefer my bed to anyone else's, this is where the emotions of the value story start. It might be tempting to share *your* feelings about the product or the opportunity, but the only emotions that matter in the value story are those of your potential customer and, as such, the identifiable character.

This is where your data, personas, and everything else you know about the people you've identified as your key customers become worth their weight in emotional gold. Take your painstaking analytics and insights and *do* something with them. Home in on the thing, the one thing your customers care most about, the thing that keeps them up at night, and tell a story that includes and taps into that emotion.

Additionally, don't underestimate the power of actually talking to your customers and prospects. Beyond online surveys and poll data, real conversations will reveal emotional nuances you might otherwise miss. Not only will you get a more intimate understanding, these conversations will give you insights as to what to include for the final two story components.

A Moment

One of the many strengths of telling a value story is that it demonstrates and, when done right, often simulates the problem you and your product solve by putting it into a specific context. While including a character and emotion will help to draw the audience into the scene, the best value stories include a specific moment in time the audience can see vividly and specifically.

The moment component can be included a variety of ways and can depend on the medium through which you are sharing the message. In the Builder.co example we used in our research, we stated a specific day and time to give the audience a sense of when exactly this occurred. This is particularly useful when the message is one-dimensional (the participants were reading the message versus watching and hearing it). In the Apple commercial, the moment was when the boy turned on the television; there was a noticeable shift and silence in that moment, signifying that something had changed.

The last thing to remember about the moment in value stories is that it's often connected to the explosion. Things had been going along as normal, and then suddenly, in this moment, things changed. It's the moment the solution is discovered, the moment the real value of the product or service is realized.

Specific Details

I was speaking at a conference for Jack Henry and Associates, a large, publicly traded tech company. They provide technology products and services to banks and credit unions that make everything we know about our relationship with our financial institution possible. Look at your statement online? Jack Henry. Make your deposits via a mobile device? Jack Henry. In July 2018, they were celebrating their biggest year yet, and as someone who works with a lot of companies, it was easy to see why. They're connected despite being dispersed. They're excited while being focused. And at the center of it all, they know that what really matters is knowing the customer. Not only does this matter once the sale is made, it matters in order to make the sale in the first place.

At the event, Steve Tomson, the general manager of sales and marketing, told his team, nearly five hundred people strong, that success depends on how well you know your customer before you even walk into the first meeting. You needed to know what they need, what they're struggling with, and how Jack Henry can help.

Customer knowledge is critical to sales, storytelling, and the value story in particular. When you tell stories to potential customers, don't be afraid to get specific with your details—think red stapler in *Office Space*. Not only will you draw them in via the co-creative process we discussed in chapter 1, but you'll be flexing your empathy muscles. If you know they likely order pizza during after-hours meetings, include that. If you know they likely have a collection of branded pens from a hundred different sales reps, include that. Each specific detail you include builds a scene that looks and feels familiar to the audience, and in doing so, they will say to themselves, "They get me."

A word of warning, though. This is a step you cannot fake. Much like the sales leader at Jack Henry said, you have to *actually know* your potential customer. Either with time, research, or experience, get to know your audience. Once you do, include details in the story you tell that will make the scene familiar and show them you really get it.

The Real Value of the Value Story

The most important characteristic of the value story is, of course, that it works. It takes terrible sales and marketing and turns it into something that can captivate, influence, and transform. The value story makes it easy for your potential client, your future loyal customer, to understand how great your product or service really is. No matter who you are or what your story is, when you shift your focus to the people you want to serve and relieve the pain they might feel or want to avoid, you'll stop having to wonder why your marketing seems flat or ineffective. Create a value story for your offering and you'll see the results. In some cases immediately.

At least, that was the case for Sara, a portrait photographer. Like many photographers, her services were pretty straightforward: she took pictures of people. Mainly senior portraits or head shots, sometimes family photos, and a very occasional wedding. Sara made money when people wanted high-quality photos. Of course, high-quality photo sessions aren't cheap, and when you consider a smartphone can take pictures that satisfy most people's photo needs, Sara was constantly trying to bridge the value gap.

One spring Sara decided to offer special Mother's Day mini-sessions. But not just any mother-baby photos. Sara wanted to take photographs of adults with *their* parents or grandparents. An interesting twist on a classic offering. Sara went about marketing it in the usual way. She put out basic advertisements on social media and elsewhere, announcing the promotion, the pricing, the times, locations, what they would get, and how to book.

Crickets.

Not a single session booked.

Needless to say, Sara was disappointed. But she refused to give up, because this was really important to her.

A few months before Mother's Day, Sara lost her grandmother. A grandmother she adored. A grandmother she lived with for ten years as an adult. A grandmother who, because of those extra ten years, Sara had the rare experience of getting to know as an adult. Not just the grandma you know as a child. A grandmother whose memory, once she was gone, prompted Sara to search every discarded cell phone and old shoebox for a photo of the two of them together from those last ten years. A decent photo with decent lighting illuminating their matching, imperfect smiles.

But those photos didn't exist.

Because Sara and her grandmother never took them.

And now Sara would give anything for the opportunity to sit down and, for thirty minutes, have a few moments captured on film with her beloved grandmother.

If only people understood *that's* what this photo shoot was about.

And that's when it hit her. She should tell that story.

So she did.

Sara rereleased the advertisements for her Mother's Day sessions, but this time, instead of focusing on what it cost or the deliverables, Sara told the story of her grandmother. The response was huge. No one questioned the cost. Instead, they shared their own stories and how deeply they connected with her story.

What was almost her biggest failure ended up being Sara's most successful portrait session ever. Bookings were double any previous sessions, all because she shared the story.

That is the essence of a value story—to illustrate value in a way nothing else can. No matter how big or small your business, if you want more sales and better marketing, start with your value stories. And if you're suddenly planning a Mother's Day photo session with your mom or grandmother, you'll have to get in line behind me.

CHAPTER FIVE

The Founder Story

How Entrepreneurs Use Story to Attract Money, Customers, and Talent

If a person asking you to invest doesn't believe her own story, why would you believe it?
—AMY CUDDY, *PRESENCE*

In 2013, I was in Las Vegas, at an event and expo for handmade artists, hundreds of whom journeyed from across the country with truckloads of bins and boxes filled with their delicate, valuable wares. Each artist set up a booth inside the football field-sized exhibition hall with the hope that when the expo officially opened and a flood of big-name buyers walked through the door, their booth would stand out enough to draw in a buyer and make a sale.

79

I arrived the evening before the event began and, as a speaker for the educational session, was offered a tour of the expo floor during setup. I strolled by endless rows of booths offering everything from delicate beads to paintings to scrap-metal statues and painted fabrics and glassware. While each booth was certainly a little different, many of them were essentially selling the same things. It wasn't long before I had distinct feelings of déjà vu. As I approached the very last row I came across a booth filled with beautiful handblown glassware. Plates, glasses, serving bowls, and platters swirled with vibrant colors. It wasn't the first glassware booth I'd seen at the expo, but it certainly caught my eye. I approached the man in the booth and greeted him partly out of curiosity and partly as an experiment to see if he'd tell me a story.

"Is this your work? It's beautiful."

"Yes. I am the artist. Thank you."

"Tell me about it . . ." I paused, smiled. "I'd love to hear more about your art. What inspires you to create it?"

He looked at me and said, "These are decorative plates."

Not exactly the answer I was hoping for, especially not from a glass-blowing entrepreneur trying to differentiate himself from the thirty other glass artists at the show. So I tried again.

"How long have you been doing this? What inspired you to start?"

"1987."

In his defense, the show hadn't yet started, so perhaps the owner/ artist wasn't in full ON mode. Whatever the reason, it was clear there would be no storytelling. Just then one of the organizers approached the booth and introduced me to the artist as "Kindra Hall, the storytelling expert presenting at the educational session tomorrow about telling your story to differentiate your brand."

Suddenly a look of recognition crossed the artist's face. As if someone somewhere had once told him he should tell his story. But before he could say anything, the organizer whisked me away. As I turned to go with her, I heard the artist call out, "Wait! Wait!" I turned and he said, "If you can, come back. I have a really great story I could tell you."

I'm sure he did.

If only he had told it when he had the chance.

Every Business Has a Story

Every business has a founder story.

Behind every business, there is a story of the *who* and the *how* it all began. A story from before the business was even a twinkle in the founder's eye. A story about the moment when an idea first struck. A story from the moment the founder realized this might actually be a business.

Whether you're in a company or you started one, this story is guaranteed. No matter how big, no matter how small, no matter how old or new—unless it's the only case of immaculate incorporation—show me a company or a product, and I'll show you a story of how it all began. There are no exceptions.

This is very good news.

Good news because, in a world that closely resembles a Las Vegas expo hall packed with rows and rows of competitors offering the exact same thing, a founder story is one of the best ways to stand out and bridge the gap between you and your potential customer.

Whether you're in the launch phase and looking to secure investor dollars or trying to differentiate yourself in a crowded, noisy market or trying to attract top talent to scale, founder stories can handle all three situations in different ways and for different reasons.

The Founder Story to Bridge the Investor Gap

Several years ago a couple of guys who had gone to college together became roommates in San Francisco. Now, I don't know if you've ever lived in the City by the Bay or know someone who has, but you're probably aware it's not known for affordable housing. San Francisco is a lot of things, but budget-friendly isn't one of them. So you can imagine, when it came time to pay rent, these guys were struggling to pull it together.

At the same time the guys were trying to pay their rent, there was a big design conference in town. So big, in fact, that all the hotels on the event's list of suggested places to stay were sold out. No room for any designers at the San Fran Inn. What were the visiting designers to do? Sleep on the streets? Sleep on the floor of strangers' homes?

Wait a minute. What if . . .

When our two poor (literally and figuratively) San Francisco roommates heard the city was sold out and there were still people looking for lodging, they got a crazy idea. What if they could rent their room to some attendees? The out-of-towners would have a place to stay, and the roommates could cover their rent with the guests' rent.

It sounded perfect—except for one major problem. The guys didn't have an extra room to rent and they certainly didn't have an extra bed. But they did have a couple of spare air mattresses and an open floor in the living room. Good enough, they decided. They'd rent those.

The roommates advertised their air mattresses and got three takers. Totally random people. And a totally awesome experience. The guests had a great time at the conference and a great time staying with the roommates, and the guys had a great time hosting them.

That's when the roommates had an idea. What if this wasn't a one-time thing? What if, instead of making rent one month, they scaled this idea and made rent every month, allowing anyone to rent their space for a random, awesome experience at the startup cost of just a couple of air mattresses?

This was the beginning of Airbnb as we know it today.[1]

And, of course, that is only part of the story. There were plenty of plot twists and creative triumphs along the way, such as:

- Financing the tough early days with credit cards and racking up tens of thousands of dollars of debt.

- Repacking cereal into "Obama O's" and "Cap'n McCain" boxes to pay off the debt and live to sell another day.
- Spreading the word by pitching bloggers with the smallest audiences, because they might give them some attention.[2]

These stories are now Airbnb lore. But what's often overlooked is just how important storytelling was to the company in its early days, back when Airbnb had just two customers, not millions, and was struggling to survive.

#startuplife

Startups always face challenges, and Airbnb had a few extra hurdles. Namely, while the idea of turning surplus home space into a business using the sharing economy seems obvious now, it wasn't at the time. Think about it. Someone says to you, "Why don't you have some strangers stay at your place this weekend? . . . What? No, they aren't friends or friends of friends. They're just strangers who found you on the internet. Maybe you can make breakfast for them too."

For many people that's an instant no, and that's how many investors responded to the idea too. Jeff Jordan is a general partner at the venture capital firm Andreessen Horowitz, a firm that, for the record, can sniff out a unicorn from a decade away. Skype, Facebook, and Twitter are just a few of their successes.

So imagine the burn when Jordan said, "The first time I heard about Airbnb I thought it was possibly the stupidest idea I'd ever heard."[3] That is a soul-crushing comment for any entrepreneur, Brian Chesky included. The only thing that likely made it easier for Chesky, one of Airbnb's founders, in the early days of the company is that Jordan's "stupidest idea" sentiment was one Chesky heard a lot.

In the first year of business, every venture capitalist Chesky pitched turned him down. As he told *Fast Company*, "People thought we were crazy. They said strangers will never stay with strangers, and horrible things are going to happen."[4]

I imagine Chesky felt the unique sense of fury and frustration reserved for those who believe in their bones they're onto something—and they actually are—but they keep getting rejected by the powers that be. Like how five-time Grammy Award–winning Lady Antebellum star, Hillary Scott, felt after being rejected on *American Idol* twice before becoming a chart topper. Or how J. K. Rowling felt after being turned down by twelve publishers for the first Harry Potter book.

In all those cases, the talent and opportunity were there. But how do you effectively communicate potential to an investor who, in the palm of their hand, holds the power to grant the opportunity of a lifetime or sign your dream's death certificate? When it comes to startups, how do you convince investors you have a business worth investing in without proof of success? How do you persuade an investor to take a risk without being able to offer much in terms of assurance? If the opportunity arises and you get the chance to stand in front of someone with pockets deep enough and faith wide enough to get your idea off the ground, what do you say?

These are good questions and ones every entrepreneur asks him or herself. The Airbnb founders weren't the first ones to ask it nor will they be the last. For some, this particular entrepreneur dilemma plays out in front of millions of people.

Sell Yourself

Every week several million viewers tune into the ABC show *Shark Tank*. And every week hopeful entrepreneurs stand before a panel of intimidating judges and pitch their idea or business or product or service in the hopes that one of the sharks will invest. Not only is it great entertainment, it sheds light (lots of lights, in fact, a whole lighting crew's worth of light) on the bridge-building challenge entrepreneurs face.

Even in the made-for-television version, the struggle is real.

Dramatic music plays as we watch the hopeful entrepreneurs march down a daunting hallway to face their fate: the opportunity of a lifetime or the end of a dream.

The pitches often start the same. The entrepreneurs introduce themselves and state the terms of the investment they seek. They briefly describe their product or business and then, well, there are a couple of options.

An obvious choice is to talk math. Armed with the knowledge that investors want to make money (and often nothing else), entrepreneurs seek ways to convince investors that saying yes to this risk is a great idea. What better way to persuade someone than with cold, hard facts? Logic is always the best policy. Rely on numbers. Things like market size and conversion rates and ROI and marginal cost. It's reassuring for the entrepreneur and sounds really official to the decision makers.

I will stop there to say it's important to have your numbers straight, but as we learned in an earlier chapter, straight numbers are almost never enough.

What is the secret formula for getting a life-changing deal?

Telling a founder story seems to be at least a part of it.

In fact, in an analysis of season six of *Shark Tank* (smack-dab in the middle of the show's run), my team coded all 116 pitches based on our story criteria and determined that 76.7 percent of the aired pitches told a story. Of those who did, more received a deal than didn't.

Perhaps part of the reason is, when it comes to a new product or idea, you're selling yourself as much as anything else.

Skeptic to Believer in One Story Flat

Although his pitch wasn't broadcast on national television, Brian Chesky and Airbnb were swimming with their own sharks as they searched for someone to grant them the funding they needed to launch what they suspected, what they knew in their bones was an incredible company.

But no amount of math in the world was going to bridge the entrepreneur-investor gap. There was an overwhelming lack of confidence in the idea, and investors just couldn't see how it would all come together. With logic leading to nothing but dead ends, the young company had no option but to turn to the power of story to convince the investors they approached. The only person who could tell that story was the founder. And the only story he had was himself.

Remember Jeff Jordan, the venture capitalist who was convinced Airbnb was the worst idea he'd ever heard? He'll stand by that claim but then add that after hearing Chesky speak, he was sold.[5]

When Jordan met with Chesky, he said, "I went from complete skeptic to complete believer in twenty-nine minutes."[6] Why? Because Chesky is a storyteller. "Every great founder can really tell a great story," Jordan told *Business Insider*. "It's one of the key things in a founder, that you can convince people to believe."[7]

With one simple story, his founder story, Chesky demonstrated what Jordan calls a founder/product fit. A story that illustrates the birth of an idea. A story that inherently says no other guy could have come across this idea at this time and in this way.

As any *Shark Tank* fan will tell you, funding an idea is about more than the idea itself. When it comes to making a bet on a company, investors are betting on not just a figurative horse but a jockey. On someone with the passion to take a company all the way to the top. Having and telling a founder story reassures investors that the founder is genuine. It's a story that generates faith beyond numbers, answers questions without effort, and fills in any missing pieces of the puzzle about where the founder has been, where the founder is going, and why this founder is worth betting on.

Whether you're in a Hollywood studio making a pitch to celebrity billionaires or in a Silicon Valley conference room, when you see the potential investors' eyes move from a stare to a laser-focused squint, it's because they're having an unspoken conversation.

Investor: Can this founder overcome adversity?

Founder: Yes.

Investor: Is this founder fully committed?

Founder: I bleed my logo colors.

Investor: Is this founder emotionally invested?

Founder: Don't tell my spouse, but our wedding wasn't the happiest day of my life. It was when I filed our articles of incorporation.

Simply hearing these answers is not enough. An investor needs to feel these answers, and knowing what we know about the effects of storytelling, a well-told founder story can give all the feels you need.

That fateful day, Brian Chesky faced one of the most intense experiences for an entrepreneur, and the thing that turned skeptics into believers was his story. It was enough to overcome any objections, create faith, and ultimately get a yes. A $112 million yes.[8]

The Founder Story to Bridge the Customer Gap

Now, I don't know if taking on investors is part of your business plan. Many founders don't use investor money and therefore don't use their founder story to secure funding. Many entrepreneurs use their own cash to drive revenue and reinvest profit to drive growth. And when I say many, I mean many.

According to the Kaufman Index, 540,000 new business owners start the entrepreneur journey each month.[9] Yes, you read that right: 540,000! A study by Intuit revealed that 64 percent of small business owners start with less than $10,000, and 75 percent of them rely on their personal savings to start their business.[10]

This means 540,000 potential competitors, 540,000 founders equally as hungry and willing to throw in their personal savings and do whatever it takes as you are. If reading this elevates your heart rate just a bit, I hear you.

As a show of support, well-meaning friends and acquaintances often send me articles or blogs or press releases about other storytelling experts, firms, or events. While I want nothing more than more people teaching and promoting the importance of storytelling, each article makes me cringe just a bit. It means competition. It means, as much as any entrepreneur would love to believe it, I am not the only one.

Whether you're in series B of funding or if, like me, you had to google what that meant, you're going to face competition and copycats. In those moments, turn to your founder story for differentiation.

Why Blend in When You Could Differentiate?

It was 2015, and Desert Star Construction founder Jerry Meek had seen it all. A third-generation builder, his favorite toy as a kid was a coffee can filled with nails and, when his father let him use it, a hammer. Looking at Jerry's portfolio answers the age-old question anyone has while paging through an upscale home magazine: Are these homes for real? Yes. Yes, they are. And Jerry builds them.

Truth be told, if Jerry were the only one who built them, there wouldn't be much of a story. But, of course, Desert Star Construction isn't the only luxury home builder. In Arizona alone, where Jerry is based and where taxes are light, the competition is steep in the luxury home-building market.

Similar to the founders of Airbnb, Jerry was confident in what he had to offer. He knew his approach was better, his team was better, and his commitment to his clients during the long building process was better. Yet he, like many business owners, was struggling to communicate his love for building and what that meant to potential clients looking to build their dream home. When he tried, it sounded like what any other builder would say. He needed a way to differentiate himself.

He needed to tell his story.

What Jerry was facing was the classic conundrum of small business owners. The company is no longer in its infancy. Purchase orders have been fulfilled; there are customers using and even loving the product or service he offers. There are systems and a team in place, and the search for new customers is no longer classified as a quest for getting started but rather a continuing effort to keep growing. It's no longer about establishment but differentiation.

Sadly, differentiation is more difficult to achieve than we'd like it to be. How do you show you're different without looking like everyone else who is claiming to be different in the exact same way?

I'm reminded of the early days of dating my husband when I would still do anything to impress him, including watching football (which you already know about) and watching *Da Ali G Show*. Yes. The show was as ridiculous as it sounds. Without trying to explain the premise, I'll tell you about one episode. The main character, played by comedian Sacha Baron Cohen, allegedly interviews a grocery store worker in the dairy aisle. Cohen points to a shelf filled with various blocks and bags of cheddar cheese and asks, "What is this?" The grocer responds, "That is cheese." Cohen takes two steps and points to another row of cheese, perhaps swiss. "And what is this?" he asks. "That is cheese," the grocer responds. Cohen takes another few steps, "And this?" He points to another cheese variation. "That is cheese." What makes the sketch funny is that, despite the fact that there are no fewer than a hundred different kinds of cheese on the shelves, they are all described the exact same way.

Different, Just Like Everyone Else

In 2012, a full two years before his business-Bible masterpiece *Essentialism* was published, Greg McKeown wrote an article for the *Harvard Business Review* titled "If I Read One More Platitude-Filled Mission Statement, I'll Scream."[11]

The article starts with a game of sorts, featuring three companies and three mission statements. The reader's job is to match the company to the mission. Seemed simple enough. The problem? The mission statements were essentially indistinguishable, interchangeable clumps of words. "Profitable growth," "superior customer service," "benefit our customers and shareholders," "highest ethical standards." The qualities they thought would set them apart actually made them indistinguishable.

I execute a similar experiment with groups that include many different companies from one industry. "How many of you use your 'commitment to excellence' as your differentiator?" The entire audience raises its hand. "How many of you claim your 'customer service' as the thing that makes you different?" The entire audience again raises its hand. "How many of you would say your 'passion' is what makes you different than anyone else?"

You get the picture.

Fortunately, when this happens there is some laughter (albeit nervous) as we collectively acknowledge our differentiators—the things that make us unlike anyone else—are exactly the same. At least in the way we're communicating them now.

This struggle to differentiate isn't just true in the cheese aisle and at industry events, it's a possible fate for any product, service, and company.

The best antidote? A founder story.

All Else Considered Equal: Story Wins

There's a reason why, when I look for garments to wear beneath my slimly tailored shift dresses, I don't buy whatever happens to be hanging on Nordstrom's shelves of solutions but always go straight for the Spanx. Why? Because I've heard Sara Blakely's story.

It's the story of how she took a chance and started a company. About how she hustled until she got a once-in-a-lifetime appointment with a buyer at a huge department store. The story of when she sat down with this buyer, and when it looked like the woman just didn't get it, Blakely convinced the woman to come to the bathroom with her to show her the product in action. Just like with Extra gum, when I'm staring at a sea of hip slimmers and waist trimmers that all pretty much promise to do the same thing, I'm going with the one whose story I love.

The same is true when I decide to splurge and get my hair blown out. No, not cut, not colored. Just dried and styled. I could walk into any salon, including the one I've been going to every six weeks for the past ten years, and get this service done. But, instead, I go to Drybar. Why? Because I've heard the founder's story. Alli Webb has told her founder story in magazines and online interviews, on podcasts, and at women's events. You name the platform or medium, and it's likely Alli has told her story there. I've heard it several times and sliced in different ways, and I'm always happy to read or hear it again. The story of her own curly hair and how that made her feel as a child (I always felt awkward as a child, not because of my hair, but I could relate). The part about overpriced blowouts (I once overdrew my bank account because I bought shampoo at the salon and didn't realize it was $100 a bottle). The part about her driving all over Los Angeles giving blowouts to her friends for cheap (I think about the number of times I spent hours writing stories for my friends' cover letters or wedding vows or acceptance speeches). The part about her brother having faith in her, encouraging her to pursue it (my husband encouraged me to quit my job to figure out how to do storytelling full time, whatever *that* meant). All the struggle, all the risk, all the leaps of faith, and eventually all the success! I mean, what more could you want?

The way my daughter smiles with wonder when Ariel turns into a human and gets to marry Prince Eric is the exact adult equivalent I feel when I hear a well-told founder story. Like, dreams *do* come true! Princesses *can* defeat the odds! It might sound as crazy as transforming from a mermaid to a human or a puppet to a real boy, but it *is* possible. The founder story blurs together with my own story, and I become a brand loyalist as a result.

Done right, the founder story does this. It taps into the desires that stir at the core of every human. No matter where the founder currently is on her or his quest for entrepreneurial success, the story of the early days often reads like a fairy tale. Which is exactly why you should tell it and never stop.

Of course, there are plenty of brands and companies to whom consumers are loyal in the absence of the founder story. But if you are a small business struggling to differentiate yourself, never underestimate the power of your founding story. Even if you've hesitated to tell it because it doesn't seem as big or exciting or dramatic as a Disney movie. When it comes to a founder story, it's not the magnitude of the story that matters; it's the decision to tell it.

Which is exactly what Jerry Meek at Desert Star Construction decided to do.

His story wasn't a big one. It wasn't a tearjerker. Hollywood probably won't turn it into a movie anytime soon. But Jerry didn't care about Hollywood; all he cared about was being able to better articulate his passion for building and why Desert Star was the best construction partner for building a dream home. To accomplish that, Jerry had to go back, way back.

He went all the way back to when he was a kid. While his friends were playing sports and G.I. Joe, he didn't do either. Instead, he built things. Real forts with slope roofs. Forts that required hammers and nails and wood. He once built a fort so big it took up half his backyard. Jerry would sit on the roof of that fort and dream about what he might build next.

Are you weeping at this point of the story? Probably not. Has this story changed your life? Likely no. That's okay, because that's not what Jerry was going for. What Jerry needed was for clients to understand he didn't casually become a builder; he was born one. If a client chose Desert Star Construction to build their home, Jerry's team would approach the project with the same sense of wonder, coupled with decades of luxury-building experience, to create a dictionary-definition dream home.

Jerry decided the best way to tell this story was via video. He would hire a crew, deliver the story direct to camera, and shoot B roll at one of his luxury construction sites to fill the visual space. It took weeks to write the script, coordinate, and finalize things. It seemed to be the perfect plan—until suddenly it wasn't.

In a twist of fate, the day the production was scheduled to commence was also the day an extremely high-profile potential client wanted to meet regarding their Personal Resort®, which would be one of the largest homes ever built in America. Desert Star Construction was one of the finalists, and Jerry was excited about the incredible opportunity. He prepared to present his pitch that afternoon, which meant the video team had a fraction of the time to get the project filmed before Jerry had to jet to make his final pitch for a project he desperately wanted to be part of.

They pulled it off. They got the footage, Jerry told his story, and no sooner did the crew say, "That's a wrap!" than Jerry was on his way to the pitch of a lifetime, which is where the real story happens. As Jerry stood in front of the client's team, ready to make his standard pitch, he remembered the fort story from the shoot that day.

In a Hail Mary decision, rather than open with a mission statement that sounded exactly like what his competition would say, Jerry told the story of building forts as a kid and how, each day, whenever he leaves a construction site, he thinks back to that first fort he built and can't help but wonder what he could build next.

Desert Star got the job.

The very, very big job.

Of course, much like the contestants on *Shark Tank*, Desert Star needed to know their stuff, to communicate they would negotiate the best prices and serve as an advocate for the client. They needed numbers, data, and proof they were exceedingly competent and excessively capable.

But in the end, when pitted against other luxury builders who could claim the exact same suite of skills, story won the day. Later on, the client specifically stated there was just something about Jerry's story, about building the fort as a kid, that made him feel Jerry's passion and trust he would deliver.

Often, all it takes is a simple story, a story of the time it all started or of the first success or the first failure. The beginning of a company is filled with stories, any number of which are unique and capable of setting you apart from everyone else. All things considered equal, your founder story will differentiate you from the competition, connect you in a meaningful way to your customer, and make you an easy yes.

The Founder Story to Bridge the Talent Gap

In addition to bridging the investor gap and the customer gap, the third gap a founder must bridge is the one that will inspire others to cross and, in doing so, become a part of the team. While a few businesses are designed to be a one-man show, more often for a business to scale and reach its full potential, a founder must bring others on. But not just any others—the best others. People who share the dream, who are invested in the outcome, and who are willing to take the wild ride along with them.

Perhaps you've heard the analogy that a draft horse can pull 8,000 pounds of dead weight, but two draft horses, with their combined power, can pull 24,000 pounds, far more than the single effort of each doubled. Whether or not that is actually true (the internet is divided on the issue), the principle remains: get the right team in place and you'll have exponentially greater success.

The problem is, good talent isn't always easy to find. And if you do find it, chances are several of your competitors have also found them. I spent much of 2017 speaking to CEOs and the key leaders of hundreds of companies in various cities across the country who were members of an exclusive mastermind group. Thousands of executives, representing companies of all sizes and across all industries, would gather for a day of networking and keynote presentations, seeking best practice takeaways and new methods of solving their biggest problems.

In 2017, no matter the city—from San Diego to Chicago, Pittsburgh to Seattle—polls showed the big problem plaguing them all was securing talent. When business is booming, the talent holds the power, and the leaders in the room all wanted to know how to get talent's attention, and the best way to persuade them to join their team and transform them into not just employees but believers.

A founder story is a great first step to getting them across that gap.

Where to Look for Your Founder Story

Of course, not every business is Airbnb or wants to be. But make no mistake, if you've started a business, you're a founder. And even though you might not think you have a founder story, you do. Guaranteed. If you're feeling insecure, just watch the stories on Kickstarter. They're real people telling their founder stories.

In chapter 8 we'll look more closely at the various strategies for finding your story, but for now I want to give you a few places where founder stories often hide and where you can find them.

Go Way Back

I was working with a group of high-performing, top-of-their-game female financial advisors. Each one was an entrepreneur. Each one was responsible for building their book of business. Each one was dedicated to serving their customers well by taking care of and helping to grow one of their customers' most prized possessions: their money. And each one was aware that the competition was stiff and their potential clients were, by default, slightly nervous. The success of each advisor was completely dependent on her ability to effectively communicate how passionate and trustworthy she was while, at the same time, differentiating herself from the nearly 250,000 other financial advisors doing the exact same thing.[12]

The solution? Finding her founder story.

To do that, many of these women went way back to when they first found their passion for money, like opening their first bank accounts or saving for their first toy.

For one woman, she remembered loving money since the very beginning. As a little girl, her favorite toy was money. Despite the fact she had a piggy bank, the money was rarely in it. The little girl loved holding it and sorting it and putting it in piles and moving it around. Any chance she got, the little girl played with her money, much to her mother's discontent.

"Don't play with money!" her mom would shout.

"Why not?" the girl would ask.

"Because!" her mother insisted in the way mothers do, as she quickly searched for a reason that would be satisfactory to a little girl. "It's dirty!" she said. "Money is dirty, and you shouldn't be playing with it."

The girl was devastated. She loved money so much, couldn't keep herself from it, but she didn't want to upset her mother. Determined, she found a solution that would satisfy both of them. The little girl went to the backyard, filled a small bucket with dish soap and warm water, and coin by coin, bill by bill, gently washed all of her money.

About halfway through the process, her mother appeared on the back stoop.

"What are you doing?!" she yelled. "I thought I told you not to play with your money!"

"You said money was dirty. But see? I'm washing it!"

At that moment the now-grown financial advisor finished the story, saying, "Of course, I know now that money laundering is not good, but my love of money has never changed. And you can be assured I will treat your money with the love and respect it deserves."

It was the beginning of the perfect founder story that she found by going all the way back to her childhood. This is the same strategy we used with the Desert Star Construction story and a strategy you can use as you begin your quest to tell your founder story.

Remember the "There Has to Be a Better Way" Moment

The day the young man left his glasses on an airplane and faced the cold, hard, soul-crushing reality of the cost of eyewear was the moment Warby Parker's cofounder said to himself, "There has to be a better way!"

If you have ever had that same realization, that same moment when you realized the way things have always been done is not the best way, you could have the beginning of a founder story.

Take some time to think about that day when the thought first hit you, the early days when you began exploring what a better way might look like. What were you feeling? Who was there? How did events unfold? Include the wonder, the disbelief. Include the parts that, in hindsight, are funny or crazy or endearing. When I say "take some time," I mean it. It's easy, as a founder, to be so immersed in where your company is right now or focused on where your company is going that you forget the moments when it all began. But some of the best founder stories are born from those "There has to be a better way!" moments.

Look for the Blood, Sweat, and Tears

It was season 5 of *Shark Tank* when a mother stood before the toothy investors. She was there to pitch her line of baby moccasins, and this mom knew her stuff. She answered every tough biz question the sharks threw her way. Margins, customer acquisition cost. They asked the question, she had the answer.

And yet the waters looked murky.

None of the sharks seemed particularly invested in investing. That is, until the Utah mother found the opportunity to tell her founder story. It wasn't necessarily about the footwear but rather about the other product she was selling: herself.

She told them what it took to get the company started. She had the idea, yes, but ideas take money, and money was something she didn't have much of. In an effort to raise enough funds to get her first products made, she spent an entire summer breaking the glass out of aluminum window frames. Grueling work, sweaty work, bloody work.

Once the frames were cleared, she brought the aluminum to a scrap yard where they gave her a total of $200. She used that $200 to buy fabric for her first few moccasins.

It wasn't until the sharks heard her story that the water in the tank turned from lukewarm to a total feeding frenzy. Because, let's face it, baby footwear, even moccasins, are not a new concept. None of the sharks cared about her baby moccasins. What they cared about was her "do whatever it takes," "sweat it out in the summer sun," "I'm not afraid of manual labor," "watch me turn $200 into millions" story. Now her moccasins are everywhere—Nordstrom, on my friends' babies—all because she told her story of blood, sweat, and tears.

When it comes to finding your founder story, don't immediately run to the sunny side of the street. Though it may be tempting to focus on your successes, you're better off looking in the shadows. Those moments that weren't all rainbows and unicorns. The Airbnb founder story isn't "We had a great idea, and we worked hard, and we were really talented and smart, and now we have a billion-dollar company." The real Airbnb story is far less glowing, and that's what makes it great.

Remember when everything was going wrong in your business? When things got ugly? When your friends and family kept saying that one line that made you want to punch them in the face: "Everything happens for a reason . . ."

Remember that?

Good.

Because that's where your story is. It's in those struggles. The bloody, sweaty, "cry it out" struggles that led to eventual victories. That's where you'll find the seeds of your founder story.

Four Founder Story Pitfalls (And How to Avoid Them)

While the founder story may appear to be a bit of a no-brainer, like the endless stream of Instagram #fail photos from when a recipe looks so easy and beautiful online but in real life turns out laughable, there are plenty of challenges, pitfalls, and ways a founder story can go wrong.

Pitfall #1: Confusing the Founder Story and the Value Story

First things first. Before we go any further, there's an important distinction to make here. The founder story is not a value story. The founder story is fundamentally about the founder. It may overlap with other stories, and it may inherently illustrate the value of the product or service being offered. But when that story becomes only about the product, it becomes a value story. As a founder, you can certainly tell a value story. But just know that they're not the same thing. When you're just talking about the product, you're selling the product, not yourself. When you're telling a founder story, first and foremost, you're selling yourself.

Pitfall #2: Not Telling Your Founder Story Because You're Tired of Telling It

For the past several years, on any given night, if you were to walk in the vicinity of West Forty-Sixth Street in New York City, you would be greeted by mass hysteria. Yes, for those who know the area, you know that West Forty-Sixth Street is Times Square, which implies chaos regardless of day or time. But West Forty-Sixth Street is special.

It's the street address for the Richard Rogers Theater. And the Richard Rogers Theater is where you go if you want to see *Hamilton* on Broadway.

Outside is mayhem: a line of people wraps around the building, nervously waiting to get in through the main entrance and hoping the $500+ tickets they bought on StubHub are legit. Inside the theater is worse. Complete and organized chaos is a generous term. Yet no one seems to mind that the line for the bathroom is one hundred people long and the price of a plastic cup of cava is $18.

Joyously, 1,319 people make their way to seats that have less legroom than the deepest-discount airline, and yet the air crackles with excitement as they prepare for the experience of a lifetime.

Meanwhile, backstage, the cast is getting ready for the show. I admit I've never been backstage on Broadway, but I bet the energy there is much less anxious than that of the audience. Think about it; the actors go to the same theater on West Forty-Sixth Street six days a week, sometimes performing two shows a day. They put on the same outfit. Sing the same songs with the same words, same notes. They walk to the exact same spot on the exact same stage in the exact same way every single show.

I don't know about you, but I sometimes get a little anxious about the natural monotony of adult life—doing the same things day in and day out. Imagine if that was your job! At what point does it drive you a little crazy? At what point do you wonder what the point of it all is? At what point do you long to sing a different song or tell a different story?

When it comes to your founder story, it's a lot like Broadway. Over time you'll get tired of singing the same notes, of delivering the same story. And because you aren't beholden to an actor's union and the next character's lines aren't dependent on yours, you'll be tempted to change it up, to not tell the story, to maybe talk about exciting new developments or new stats instead. New anything! Anything but the same old notes you're tired of singing.

But in those moments, think about those actors on Broadway. And how, though the lines are always the same, they understand their performance isn't about them. It isn't for them. Those actors step onstage each night to tell the same story to the 1,319 new people sitting in the Richard Rogers Theater, eager to experience *Hamilton* for the very first time.

Just like an actor on Broadway or a preacher from the pulpit who only has the same old 2,700-year-old material to work with, your story might feel tired to you from time to time. When this happens, shift your focus from you to them.

Yes, the story might be about you, but telling it is not. It might sound old to you, but to the person hearing it for the first time, it's as new as the day it happened, and your audience will love hearing it.

Pitfall #3: Thinking You Can't Tell the Founder Story When You're Not the Founder

I understand this chapter is geared toward the founders of companies, the entrepreneurs, the ones who got the whole thing started. But I would be remiss if I didn't acknowledge there's a good chance you are not a founder. There is a chance you are a committed member of a team or leader for the cause who, though you aren't responsible for founding the company, you're still connected to the founder story and understand the importance of telling it.

For you, I have this to say: anyone can tell a founder story. And the hope is everyone does! Even if you weren't the one who got the whole thing going, even if you are employee number 3304, if you know the founder story, you have my permission (okay, my plea) to tell it. The secret is this: the story stays the same, only the transition into the story changes a bit.

Instead of saying, "I'll never forget the day I started this company" (which is a pretty rough way to start a founder story in the first place, but let's just go with it), start your story with, "I remember the day I heard the story of how it all began here at XYZ." Then tell a little bit about the circumstances of when you heard the story. Was it during your interview? Did you read it online in advance?

Then say, "The story, as I was told, started . . ." And then transition into telling the founder story as it's usually told, except instead of telling it in first person (*I* felt this, *I* did that), use third person (*he* felt this, *she* did that).

Finally, once you finish the founder story as it's typically told, add a line or two about your experience to wrap it all up. Something like, "When I heard that story I knew [insert important, relevant insight], and I hope you feel that too." Done!

Founder stories need as many voices telling the story as possible. Never let the fact that you weren't the one who started it keep you from telling the story of how it all began.

Pitfall #4: Letting the Reluctant Founder Shut Down the Founder Story

I received an email from a woman after a conference I spoke at. She worked in the marketing department of a company with a great founder story, and she was desperate to tell it.

The problem? The founder refused to let her.

If this sounds familiar to you, let me start by saying, I feel for you.

101

It can be challenging when you aren't the founder and you know there is a great founder story to tell. Yet unlike the previous section, instead of figuring out how to tell it yourself, you're struggling to get it told at all.

This is not uncommon. Founders, particularly those from the generations prior to Generation X, are often hesitant to share their story. The reasons range from the belief that a company figurehead talking about starting a company looks dated and self-glorifying (which, yes, if done wrong, a founder story can look rigid, bloviated, and even cheesy) to insisting that the story isn't about them but rather "the people and the company and the customers."

I physically cringed as I wrote that last sentence.

Anytime a founder gives you one of these as reasons not to share their story, whatever you do, *do not* accept them. Because while those sound like perfectly noble reasons not to tell a founder story, they are irrelevant.

First, if you follow the format outlined in this book, if you include the essential components (the genuine emotions, the hope and disappointment, and everything else you've learned thus far), the story will not be self-aggrandizing but endearing. People want to do business with people, and hearing the founder story reminds them that, yes, behind the website, the marketing, the spot price on the stock exchange, there is an actual person who started it all.

It may take some time and some coaxing. It may take several attempts and significant efforts to move your founder beyond the typical company speak: "We believe in excellence and integrity . . . blah blah blah." But I encourage you to keep working at it. Keep looking for moments that could work as an explosion in the story. And when you find it, write the story for them. Remember, our stories don't sound like stories to us. Our stories just sound like life. Your founder's story isn't going to sound like a story to them; they will only realize there's something really beautiful there after you tell the story to them.

And that, I must say, is one of the greatest honors of being a storyteller for others. That moment when you tell their story back to them and they had no idea it was even there.

The Founder Story: Breaking Down the Components

Whether you are looking to raise capital, secure more clients and customers, or recruit your dream team, telling a story is your solution.

And not just any story. A founder story.

Fortunately, when you include the essential storytelling components, this story basically writes itself. Let's take a look at how the four components look in the context of the founder story.

Identifiable Characters

At its core, the founder story, as you might have guessed, centers around the founder. It's designed and told to position the entrepreneur as the right captain for this idea's ship. So when it comes to identifiable characters, it might seem obvious that the founder is it. Putting the founder front and center is the only way we get to know you, believe in you, and root for you.

Obvious.

And yet this is where many founder stories go wrong.

A few years ago our team was approached by a founder who had a desire to tell his company's story. They had everything you could want from a company: a passion for the work they do, a genuine commitment to creating excellent products and services, and as icing on the cake, they were frustrated that other companies in their space were beating them in sales and social equity with inferior products.

We were excited about this project for many reasons, but particularly because we suspected we were just one great founder story from rising above the proverbial noise. In highly saturated markets like this one, when everyone is pretty much saying the same thing, given time, a well-executed founder story can elevate a brand powerfully.

Unfortunately, the ending of this story is not a happy one.

After weeks of interviews, drafts, and revisions, we were at a standstill. The problem? The founder didn't want the story to have people in it.

The first draft of the story was a classic founder story with the identifiable character as the founder himself, as it should be. He rejected that version, saying he didn't want the story to be about him. In another version, in an effort to creatively work around this roadblock, we focused on a different character and used other components to tap into that essential, pitch-winning founder story vibe. He scratched that one too. Ultimately, he didn't want the story to have people in it. He wanted the story to be about a "commitment to excellence" and "better ingredients," which, as you might have guessed, was exactly what his competition was saying.

The great strength of the founder story is that an identifiable character is a gimmie. And since people—investors, customers, potential talent—want to work with people and not faceless companies, having a built-in character like the founder is a win-win.

Unfortunately, my team and the company could not come to an agreement on this, and we mutually parted ways. I'd tell you who they are, but it wouldn't really matter, because you've never heard of them.

Authentic Emotion

As we learned from our research, including emotion in your story is essential to making it more relatable, compelling, and sticky. Simply stating the order in which things occurred will not connect with an audience in any meaningful way.

When it comes to the founder story, your first step to adding emotion is to consider what the respective audience cares about. What do you want them to feel or know as a result of hearing this story? Here are a few examples.

Investors care most about whether or not you can survive the trials and tribulations that come with starting a company. They want to know you can handle adversity, that you aren't a starry-eyed shell, that you've felt the sting of defeat and bounced back with more determination. When preparing your story for investors, include some of the negative emotions you've experienced: frustration, betrayal, doubt. They need to know you've felt these things and worked through them.

That being said, the key to the founder story for investors is to balance those negative emotions with what positive emotions grew from them: determination, relief, pride. The contrast between these emotions is what makes a founder story great.

Customers care most about your connection to the product, the service, and your commitment to creating a better life for them. They care that you're human, that behind the logo and the price tag is a person with a dream or a solution. This is not unlike telling your story to investors. Include how it felt to survive the highs and lows of creating the company.

But slightly different from crafting your story for investors, when telling the story to potential customers, include the emotions of what drove you to create this solution in the first place. What were you frustrated by? What problem were you dealing with? The Airbnb founders couldn't pay their rent and were looking for a solution to make ends meet. The fear of not being able to pay your essential bills is real for many of the Airbnb customers who rent out their spaces. Including that side of their founding story resonates with the customers who are looking to make additional income and have never realized the unused space in their home could do it.

New talent cares most about your passion for your work. They want a founder who is committed, enthusiastic, and loves what she or he does. Passion is contagious. When you tell your founder story to new team members, it should include love—the kind of love that twinkles in the eye of a new father or a woman who has just met the one. Instead of "boy meets girl," it's "founder makes company."

Of course, none of these emotions are mutually exclusive. Investors and customers want to know you have passion for what you do; new talent wants to know you've faced challenges and survived. Your founder story should be consistent, and traces of your emotions should be a part of the story regardless of the audience. But if you want to play one over the other, it's a super-pro move.

A Moment

The easiest, most-often overlooked component of the founder story is the moment. Many neglect to identify a specific point, place, or moment and instead make a broad-stroke allusion to time in general. To avoid this unnecessary mistake, as you're crafting your story, include a specific moment, like sitting at your desk for the first time, watching your first order come in on the internet, or turning the sign on your door from "closed" to "open." Say something like, "I'll never forget the day . . ." or "I'll never forget the first time . . ." or "I remember when . . ." as a way to segue into the moment. Even something as simple as a date, a day of the week, or the weather outside will satisfy your audience's need for a moment.

Specific Details

As we've discussed, details are audience-specific. Depending on what you know about the audience to whom you are telling your founder story, you will include different pieces to help them connect their experience with yours. Rely on details universal to your audience. If your customers are new parents, include a specific detail new parents can relate to. If your audience is new talent, include a specific detail about what it feels like to be a part of something you truly care about.

Ultimately, what makes a founder story inherently familiar is the reality of being human. It's not about numbers. It's not about market share. It's not about logos and social media strategies. The founding of a company is about a person on a path, and whether it's the path we make, the path we choose, or the path that happens to be there at the time, path navigating is what being human is all about.

No Second Chances

Ultimately, the power of a founder story is its ability to humanize the business the founder started. To remind people that behind the building or logo or bank statement is a person who started it all. Regardless of if you're the founder or if you work for a company whose founding story is amazing, my hope is you choose this story as your default opener. Instead of leading with facts, figures, or information, the story needs to start with the people behind the company.

After all, if you don't start there, you often don't get a chance to go there at all.

Except in the case of the glassblower at the 2013 Las Vegas handmade artist expo. You know, the one who told me what year the company started and that the glass bowls were, indeed, glass bowls (thank you, Captain Obvious). He learned I was a storyteller just as I was walking away from him, and he tried to call me back because he had a great story to tell.

Recognizing the meta-storytelling opportunity, I revisited the booth the next day. And this time he told me the story.

His parents had wanted him to be a lawyer. They weren't overt about it, but there was always some subtle pressure to pursue a career in law and all it came with: prestige, security, money. But the truth was, the man had always known he was an artist. He was happiest when he was creating things, thriving in all of his artistic pursuits. Nevertheless, not wanting to let his parents down—he shrugged, knowing it was a classic tale—he went to law school and got a job at a local practice. He did fine. He did well actually. He was pretty good at it. But he hated it. Long hours, joyless work. He hated every minute.

To offset the misery, he turned to crime.

He smiled as he let that last statement settle in. I mean, I know you're not supposed to judge a book by its cover, but this soft-spoken, middle-aged guy with curly silver hair, unsuspecting glasses, and kind smile did not scream hardened criminal.

His crime of choice: stealing scraps of discarded glass.

On his way home each night from the law office, he passed a glass manufacturing warehouse. Because he worked such long hours, and because it was always way past regular work hours before he was heading home, the glass company was usually closed up for the night. And their garbage containers were unattended. So every night the man would stop and dig through the glass company's trash to pull out pieces of glass they had thrown away. He took them to his garage and, working into the wee hours of the morning, taught himself how to create the pieces I currently saw on display.

"And now this is what I do." He gazed around the booth, a subtle look on his face that reminded me of a father presenting his children with a sweet sense of pride and satisfaction. A look I'm not sure his father ever gave him, but a look that made it not matter.

"Thank you," I said. "Thank you for sharing that story with me."

"Thank you for coming back to hear it. I'd forgotten that story."

One of the easiest stories to forget to tell is the founder story, because amid all the other drama of what it takes to get a company off the ground, it's easy for this story to get lost in the shuffle. When it comes to business, stories don't often sound like stories; they just sound like part of a start-up life. But overlooking the founder story means missing a powerful opportunity to connect with investors, to differentiate yourself from the competition, and eventually secure talent for a thriving team. The glassblower asked me to come back to hear his story and I did. But more often than not, you don't get a second chance to tell the story.

———

Successful founders, like those of Airbnb, eventually go on to become more than that. Their fledgling businesses grow into something bigger, something with a life of its own. More customers arrive. More employees arrive. Two guys in a garage become a tech giant. Three air mattresses on the floor become hundreds of thousands of beds around the world. What was once a small, nimble, unpredictable start-up becomes an organization.

When that happens, founders transition too. Yes, they'll always be founders, but now they're something else: they're leaders.

And that, as they say, is a whole different story.

CHAPTER SIX

The Purpose Story

How Great Leaders Use Story to Align and Inspire

Stories constitute the single most powerful weapon in a leader's arsenal.

—HOWARD GARDNER, HARVARD UNIVERSITY

I t was July 2008.

More than two hundred salespeople from around the world had gathered in a hotel ballroom to learn about new products, gain new sales insights, and celebrate their successes. It was always the highlight of the year: a huge party, a lot of whoop-whooping and rah-rahing and way-to-go-ing. And this event would be no different, except—

Read that first line again.

It was July 2008.

Anyone in sales, particularly those in 100-percent commissioned sales, heck, anyone in the United States, will tell you that 2008 was not a year for celebrating. A year for consoling? Yes. A year for cutting back? Yes. But a year for celebrating? Let me ask you, how well do you think a round of rah-rahing would go over at a funeral? Right. That was 2008.

And while the reality of 2008 was painful for everyone, it was particularly complicated for one member of the executive team, a young man you already know, my now-husband Michael. Since 2002, he had been working behind the scenes for the company as their finance guy. He worked tirelessly, as finance guys do, to keep the company's books straight and its cash flow healthy and to serve as a strategic partner to the owners as they navigated the somewhat tumultuous financial landscape. Michael was good at his job, so good in fact that the owners decided to give him a more front-facing role. Why keep this secret weapon a secret?

As the ball dropped, marking the end of 2007 and the beginning of a brand-new year, Michael's role shifted, and his official coming-out party was scheduled for the July 2008 annual sales event. There he was given thirty minutes to simultaneously introduce himself as an emerging leader and deliver a state of the union–type address.

For the owners, this was an opportunity for their new leader to make a splash and rally the sales force for the coming year.

For Michael, it was a daunting minefield of problems.

When things are going great, this kind of speech isn't that difficult. The stakes are low and morale is high. When you're helming a thriving organization in a booming economy, you can get up and more or less bullhorn your way through with something akin to, "I'm super stoked to be here! You guys are the best! You killed it last year, and we're going to kill it twice as hard this year!" In essence, you can do the keynote equivalent of a double fist pump and high-five and walk off the stage to a round of applause.

But in this case, the market was failing, the sky was falling, and

Michael would be addressing, if not a crew on a sinking ship, then at least a very hostile and anxious crowd. A fist pump had a better chance of creating a fistfight than any applause.

Michael knew better than anyone the challenges they were facing. He was a numbers guy, after all. He had already determined that a "go get 'em" speech would not only sound empty, it might do more harm than good. With the company facing some seriously troubled waters, he needed to connect with an uncertain, skeptical audience at a deeper level.

What they needed wasn't a state of the union speech or some cheerleading routine. What they needed was a story.

A real, raw, authentic story.

A story that gave them a reason to stay, to keep at it, to not quit, although all signs pointed to a need to jump ship.

What Michael needed was a purpose story.

The Purpose Story

A quick recap: there are four key story types that drive business success. So far we've examined the value story, which describes how your product or service impacts the user. The second is the founder story, used to increase stakeholder faith in the person who created the company. Those two stories are almost always the first to be told in business—they're the things that come into existence first in a business. Invariably, entrepreneurs and the value they're trying to bring to the world are the first stops on the business journey.

As a business grows, however, one thing always happens: new people arrive. Employees, contractors, temps, and freelancers begin to fill out the ranks of the growing venture. Those new people are critical to growing a company. Beyond a certain size, you simply can't grow without more people. But new people pose a problem too: they're not the founder. They don't have the same skills, aren't driven by the same motivation, and frequently don't understand as clearly what the company does or why.

Aligning what can eventually amount to a small army of people and inspiring them to take action every day is a daunting but critical task, one that leaders would be wise to turn to storytelling for. The purpose story offers members of an established organization a reason to show up each day. To commit, to cooperate, and to accomplish something together.

Purpose Over Profit

Remember Paul Zak? He's the oxytocin guy who taught us about the importance of trust and reciprocity. He observed, "We know that people are substantially more motivated by their organization's transcendent purpose (how it improves lives) than by its transactional purpose (how it sells goods and services)."[1]

Transcendent versus transactional purpose. At the end of the day, people in your organization might be excited about what it is you're selling, but they're going to be far more excited about why. That's what's at the heart of the purpose story and how leaders can bridge the gap for their teams.

Research supports this idea. Companies that have a stated purpose other than profit, and that align themselves with it, return more profits over time. It can seem counterintuitive, but in the absence of a purpose, profit steps in to fill the void.[2]

Think Toms shoes with their buy-one-give-one approach. Or Bombas socks with the same promise. Or Warby Parker with giving as much as they sell. Think about it. If a sock company, a shoe company, and an eyeglass company can be about saving the world one foot and eyeball at a time, what does that say about humans and business?

We really, really need *why* in our lives.

Part of our need for purpose may be wired into us. We have an almost inescapable habit as humans to want to give meaning to things. From an evolutionary perspective, being goal-oriented and purpose-driven is an advantage. Wandering aimlessly versus hunting and gathering, for example, deliver entirely different results. Both involve walking, but with the first one, you starve to death.

We're wired to want purpose and to give meaning to things. It's part of why story matters, but it's also why purpose matters so much in work. In a vacuum, we'll attribute meaning where none exists. We do the same thing at work. People want a purpose. If you don't give them one, they'll make up their own. Tell your stories first, otherwise someone might tell them for you, and you might not like their version.

The Purpose of the Purpose (Story)

Enter the purpose story. One of the most versatile of our story types, purpose stories can bridge all kinds of internal company gaps. At their core, purpose stories are about alignment and inherent inspiration. And the larger an organization gets, the more those two things matter. Together, alignment and inspiration create purpose, and you need both to make progress. Fortunately, a purpose story can align teams in a variety of ways and for a variety of reasons.

Alignment Around a Goal or Initiative

Researchers have long studied the effects of storytelling as a means by which humans connect and organize themselves and their understanding of the world. Recently, researchers wanted to explore the impact of storytelling within a team: in particular, a story's impact on team mental models and the way in which members understand relevant information. More alignment means enhanced team processes and improved performance.[3] In short, the researchers wanted to determine if teams would function better, solve problems more cohesively, and collaborate in more effective ways if stories were a part of the preparation process.

To test this, and a variety of other hypotheses, researchers divided participants into groups of three and had the groups participate in a series of online simulations where each member was assigned a role as a police officer, fire fighter, or hazmat worker. The simulations were a mock crisis situation wherein the members of the group were tasked with addressing "the release of an airborne chemical on campus."[4] Group members had to work together to efficiently and effectively solve the problem.

To test the effects of storytelling, half of the groups watched an instructional video that included a story about a mishap in a chemistry lab and a student who was seriously injured because the response team did not coordinate themselves. The control groups watched a video that simply stated the importance of collaboration and timing but did not include a story to illustrate the importance of those points.

In the end, the teams who were told the story were "more similar in their view on how events should be solved than teams who were given the same message in a nonstory format,"[5] and the use of stories was the more effective approach to getting everyone on the same page.

The results of the study aren't surprising. Storytelling, as a method for uniting, clarifying, and motivating groups of people, has been used for years and for many different goals and initiatives both in and outside of business.

———

I was sitting in a hotel room in Philadelphia the Tuesday evening of the 2018 midterm elections. I ordered room service, sat on the bed, and out of curiosity, changed the channel back and forth between the two major news stations for the two different parties. And though the commentary about each nomination was completely opposite depending on if an outcome went red or blue, one thing was indistinguishable: both sides repeatedly mentioned the stories the various candidates told during their campaigns. Both sides acknowledged the power of the stories that were told and the glaring absence when a story was not told.

Of course, political endeavors are just one way stories are used to align and motivate. I think about the team that goes into a locker room at halftime several points behind and the story a coach must tell to inspire a win. I think of the hundreds of GoFundMe profiles I've read whose stories are designed to inspire donations to bring dreams to life. I remember a workshop I facilitated where the company's number-one goal was to ensure team members followed a safety protocol and how sharing stories of the devastating times protocol wasn't followed helped keep the team committed to the goal.

If you have a team to unite and, for whatever reason, are struggling to do it, a purpose story is likely the bridge you've been searching for.

Alignment Around a Sensitive Subject

I spoke at the national sales conference for a large tech company. My session was scheduled for midmorning, but I made my way to the ballroom early so I could sit in on some of the other keynotes, namely, those delivered by the company executives. I found one of the last remaining seats in the packed ballroom and settled in just in time for the vice president of sales to take the stage. He was obviously well respected, and he opened his state of the state address with a story.

He told us that his oldest daughter was just about to graduate high school, and he had a distinct sense that his days of imparting fatherly wisdom upon her were quickly coming to a close. So he decided to set up a special date night just for the two of them. The audience laughed as he described the unfolding events. His daughter chose the most expensive restaurant in town. The first time she came downstairs, he made her change because her outfit was inappropriate for the restaurant she had chosen. How she sneered at the bread basket and barely touched her meal, mumbling something about wanting to fit into her prom dress.

Undeterred, he continued with his plan to bestow wisdom. "Though I did make a slight adjustment in that, instead of bestowing *all* my wisdom, I would just bestow one piece of wisdom." The audience laughed along with him, empathizing with the poor, clueless dad. As soon as the waiter removed the appetizer, the man told his daughter the importance of paying attention to detail. "In all things," he said. "In your classes. In your work-study. In your friendships. In your romantic relationships."

He looked at her, and she didn't even try to disguise her disinterest. Nevertheless, he persevered.

Twenty minutes of the "pay attention to the details" lecture later, and he still had no reaction from his daughter. He finally broke. "Honey," he said, "is it me, or are you not even listening to me?!" She gave him a dead-pan stare. "I'm trying to bestow . . ." He caught himself. "I'm trying to teach you how important the details are, that details really matter!" He couldn't hide his agitation. "And I feel like you don't even care!"

He stopped.

She stared at him.

He raised his eyebrows, signaling to her. "Well, say something."

She rolled her eyes and said. "It's really hard to take you seriously, Dad, when you're talking about how important it is to pay attention to the details, but you are wearing two different socks." She paused. "Just sayin'."

The ballroom was quiet, the audience collectively shared in the pain of falling off a self-righteous horse. The vice president smiled sheepishly and admitted his daughter was right and, more importantly, that the company had been guilty of a similar sin, saying one thing and doing another. "I understand that our house can feel divided at times, that there's the corporate office and you, our dedicated reps. And that we at headquarters often give mixed messages. We preach to you the impor-tance of deepening the relationships with current clients but then only reward you when you bring in new ones." Even in the darkened ballroom, I saw the reps exchanging glances.

"I want to apologize for that," he said. "And to promise that, in the future, we will be more consistent, that what we say will also be what we do.

"And as for my daughter," he smiled, "something tells me she'll be just fine at college. With or without my wisdom."

I couldn't believe it. It was the perfectly executed purpose story. Not too dramatic, totally relatable, and illustrating the point perfectly. Sure, he could have stood on stage and talked about company initiatives or said, "We're committed to listening to the field more." But much like Michael, in the story at the beginning of this chapter, those words are risk-level-red for sounding empty and trite.

Instead, this executive chose a story to help frame an awkward conversation. By recounting another time when he realized his missteps, the audience was open to hearing the message as a whole.

Alignment Around What You're Really About

Sodexo loves food.

The culinary division of the food service giant wants you to know that. Well, yes, they want *you* to know that, but they really want their customers and potential customers to know that. And when they're recruiting more chefs to cook in their kitchens across the globe, from corporate offices to hospitals to attractions and beyond, they want the chefs to know that Sodexo shares their love and passion for food.

The problem, of course, is that just saying, "We have a passion for food" or "We love food" isn't enough. Sodexo wants people to feel their love. They want to move people. They want to leave no question that, when it comes to food, Sodexo is about more than what is on the profit and loss sheet. Sodexo loves food.

How could they communicate this driving purpose?

You might have guessed it. By telling a purpose story.

The story came to us at a storytelling workshop in 2016 and was further developed, scripted, and eventually turned into a short video by the talented team at Seattle-based film company LittleFilms in 2017.

During the workshop, the one-hundred-person audience broke into smaller groups, and each group was responsible for finding and creating a story that could illustrate some of their most critical messages about what the culinary excellence team is really about. One group was tasked with tackling the concept of a love of food. After tossing around various ideas, one man, a chef, told a story of his love of food.

As an eight-year-old boy in New Delhi, he remembered a house filled with family—his parents, aunts, uncles, and cousins. So many people going different directions. It was loud and chaotic and filled with joy.

Each night they all sat down at the table to eat. For that hour every night they shared their different stories from the day, their different dishes, and their different dreams.

Looking back, he thought those experiences, those meals together with his family, might be the reason he became a chef—but not for the reasons we might think.

About the time he turned thirteen, everyone started to move away. The mealtimes, the stories, everything changed. For years after that, he obsessed over learning the recipes from those earlier days, those dishes he'd had as a young boy at that dining table in New Delhi. But though he could recreate the food, it never tasted the same.

It wasn't until now that he understood why.

Because now, on the days when he takes a moment to look up from his work, he sees a familiar sight: so many people going in so many different directions but stopping to eat his food; chefs laughing, working, cooking; a loud and chaotic scene filled with joy. Suddenly, he is back in New Delhi, back at the table, having dinner with his family.

And then he realized why, after so many attempts, he hadn't been able to recreate the memories through recipes alone.

Because food is more than ingredients. The love of food comes from time together. From people sharing stories and dreams. There was a time when he thought being a chef was about creating food. Today, he knows being a chef is about creating an experience, and that is what he gets to do every day at Sodexo.

When Raj, the chef, shared that story in front of the whole group at the workshop, there wasn't a dry eye in the place, including mine. And though the mood the entire day had been positive and upbeat, there was a notable shift after he shared—a deeper pride, a bigger meaning to what they were all there to do.

Yes, they all knew with their brains that Sodexo loves food. But it wasn't until hearing that chef's story that they felt what that meant. And connected to it. And were invigorated by it. After the workshop I received many compliments and accolades from the people who were in the room, but I knew it was that story and the others that were shared, not the six hours of content I delivered, that made that workshop the fulfilling, purposed-filled event it ended up being.

A single purpose story has the ability to unite entire teams of people and reconnect them to the deeper meaning of their work.

The Key to a Successful Purpose Story

When it comes to telling a successful purpose story, there is one thing that matters more than anything else, more than the components, more than the details you include. Purpose stories live and die on how well, how strongly the story supports a specific message. The purpose story is dependent on, first, the clarity of that message and, second, how clearly the story illustrates that message.

In other words, all purpose stories start with this essential question: What point do I want to make? Said another way: What do I want my audience to think, feel, know, or do as a result of hearing this story?

The answer to that question is your North Star. It's what will guide you when you decide which story to develop. It'll determine which pieces of a story you keep and which pieces you cut because of time or relevance.

You remember the team at the Maricopa Medical Center in chapter 2, the ones trying to raise funds for their foundation who relied on true, heartfelt stories to drive donations. Well, before the giving began, before dinner was served, the new CEO was tasked with delivering a speech. It was supposed to be a state of the state address. But he was the new CEO of an organization dealing with a bit of turmoil, and the speech had to be so much more than that. It had to be a purpose story. It was his one chance, with the most important stakeholders in the room, to communicate in a real, authentic, and moving way why they should all continue to believe—to believe in him, yes, but more importantly the institution as a whole.

The point he wanted to make? They should all be proud of what their organization is and what it stands for: quality health-care for the otherwise forgotten, compassion for the most vulnerable.

With that as our due north, we got to work, and with a little digging, we found the perfect story to connect the attendees with their purpose. When the night of the event and fund-raiser came around, instead of opening the evening with statistics, the CEO told a story.

It was the story of one of his first events as the new CEO, a town hall discussing the bond they were hoping would pass to provide desperately needed funding. It took place in the multipurpose room of a community building, with metal folding chairs assembled in rows and a table in the back set up with water bottles and store-bought cookies. The CEO remembered watching people file in and take their seats, and then, as a speaker welcomed those who had gathered and the CEO prepared to take the stage, he noticed something out of the corner of his eye. A man shuffling into the room.

It was clear, even from a distance, that this man lacked any resources. Homeless perhaps. Whether he intended to be there for the meeting or just happened to stumble across a crowd and wanted to check it out, the CEO wasn't sure. Either way, the man shuffled to the front of the room and stopped just shy of where the speaker stood.

Now, anywhere else, in anyone else's public forum, some staff would have approached the disheveled man and escorted him to the door with whispers of "This event isn't really for you" while everyone else in the crowd shifted uncomfortably in their seats, hoping the man would leave without causing a scene.

But that was not so at this forum.

Yes, several people rose to their feet and quickly made their way to the man, but not to shoo him away. One brought him a bottle of water. Another brought him a metal folding chair so he could sit. And someone brought him a napkin with several assorted cookies.

When the CEO got to this part of the story, he paused slightly to let the scene sink in. The room of potential donors at the fund-raiser didn't even let out a breath. The CEO resumed his speech, mentioning a few recent accolades, briefly including the kind of information the audience likely expected from a fund-raiser's opening address. But long before anyone could so much as clear their throat, the CEO returned to the story of the disheveled man.

"I think back to that evening of the forum. I think about the man who had been turned away by the rest of the world. But you—our people, our Maricopa community—you gave him a few moments of dignity with something as simple as a bottle of water and a handful of cookies. And it is in these moments you leave your legacy. Thank you for a wonderful first year. I am humbled and proud to be in your presence each day."

That was it.

He stepped away from the podium to uproarious applause from an audience who, I'm convinced, still wasn't exactly sure what had just happened. The emcee thanked him and then welcomed the audience to enjoy dinner and "the special cookie that has been placed at each of your seats."

With one story matched to a crystal-clear message, the new CEO united the somewhat skeptical stakeholders, and the overall purpose prevailed.

A Word of Warning

All this being said, there is a flip side to purpose story success: there is very little room for error when it comes to matching the message, the ultimate point you want to make, with the story you end up telling.

By nature, the main character of a purpose story (as we'll learn in the components section of this chapter) is typically the leader who is telling the story. Which is fine and exactly as it should be. But because this is indeed the case, and because, by default, you are in some position of leadership in the company to even be granted the opportunity to tell a purpose story (Are you following this?), if you tell a story that doesn't perfectly illustrate your message, if you tell a story that leaves your listener wondering, *What was the point of that?* you will have committed the ultimate storytelling crime: telling a story for the story's sake. Not meticulously matching your story to your message could backfire in extremely detrimental ways. Instead of being perceived as an inspirational leader, you run the risk of being labeled an arrogant one.

Now, of course, haters gonna hate, but spending extra time to ensure that, at the end of your story, the team better understands the actual initiative or mission or objective will save you a whole lotta hurt.

Purpose Story Hack

It sounds easy, right? Just clarify your message and find a story to match. What's the big deal? And yet, if you've ever tried it, it's a lot harder than it seems. Don't be discouraged if you've tried to tell a purpose story before and couldn't because, though you had the message, you could never seem to get your hands on a story. Although there are no shortcuts in life and a free lunch is never free, there is a simple way to uncover your purpose story and lure it out of the mental caves in which it tends to hide.

Once you're clear on the message you want to deliver, the next step is to ask yourself: When did I learn this lesson? When did I discover this truth?

Let's return to the vice president of sales of the tech company who wanted to deliver the message that sometimes corporate says one thing but does another and that's a problem. When he asked himself the question, "When have I learned this before?" the story about dinner with his daughter emerged. For the CEO of the Maricopa Medical Center who wanted his message to unite his stakeholders with pride in what they're really there to do, he asked himself, "When have I seen our true purpose in action?" He recalled the homeless man who had been treated with respect.

For Michael, the young executive from the beginning of this chapter who was just moving into a sales role during a nationwide financial crisis, his message was "I know things are hard, but if you give up, you'll regret it."

When did he learn that lesson? His senior year of college on the water polo team.

———

When the time came for Michael to take the stage at his company's conference, he was prepared but nervous. He knew his approach wasn't going to be what the audience expected, especially not at a sales conference and especially not from a former finance guy.

He waited for the emcee to introduce him, and nerves and all, he took the stage and prepared to give his first speech since high school English class. A speech that started with a story from high school.

It was his freshman year. Michael was walking across campus on one of the first days of school when a teacher called to him from across the courtyard. It was the water polo coach. Michael realized the coach was talking to him. "Hey," he said, "how tall's your dad?"

"Uh, six foot six or something," Michael murmured the way only a high school student can.

"You need to play water polo," the coach said.

Michael expressed humility and disbelief as he related the way in which he was recruited to play a sport he'd never tried and knew little about. He told the audience the coach, in an effort to persuade Michael further, took him to the Division I collegiate water polo championship game between UCLA and Stanford.

Michael recounted sitting in the stands and, from those cold metal bleachers, watching the athletes in the pool with admiration and deciding then and there not only to play water polo but to someday play in the championship game.

Of course, a possible college championship was years away, which meant time was on his side. This worked in Michael's favor as he started working through a few minor details that stood in his way: not knowing what an eggbeater was (the swimming kind, not the baking kind) and a slight distaste for Speedos, to name two. Unwilling to let those stop him, Michael got to work.

From that moment on Michael was the first one into the pool and the last one out. He survived hell weeks and two-a-days and then hit the gym to lift weights. He also worked on his mental shape. Michael was a self-proclaimed hothead, so he worked to manage his temper and channel those emotions toward sharper play.

It took a lot of time, a lot of work, but eventually it paid off.

During his junior year, Michael became captain of the team, his first true leadership position. In his senior year he was recruited to play for UCLA. Everything was going according to plan.

At this point, Michael paused. Not for dramatic effect, but because this is where things got real. He took a breath. "When I got to college, things changed. The level of play was higher. The guys were bigger and better. I had to work harder. I had to gain more weight, more muscle, more everything."

At first, he did what he needed to do. But gradually he began to slip. He was no longer the first in the pool and the last out. His attention and commitment waivered. He knew it was going to be hard. He wasn't afraid of hard, but this was a little harder than he had bargained for.

One day the coach called him in and said, "Look, I've got guys that are younger than you, faster than you, and care more than you. You need to step up or step off the team."

It was Michael's senior year. He was kind of over it. So he quit.

"Looking back at those days in college," Michael explained to a rapt audience, "I realize now that they were kind of like the downturn in a business. A part of the natural ebb and flow of life. But at the time, I didn't have the experience or the maturity or the good sense to realize that a hard period is actually an opportunity to rise above and move ahead."

At this point, you could hear a pin drop in the room. Michael moved to the front of the stage.

"I was fourteen years old when I set my sights on that championship game, watching the players and vowing to be in that pool someday."

He breathed again.

"There I was. Seven years later. Seven years of hard work, of constant improvement, and one decision to quit later, and I found myself back in the stands, watching my team win the national championship—from the cold, metal bleachers."

He shook his head slightly.

The audience swallowed hard.

The lesson Michael learned that day is one that any of us needs on any given day, but on that day in 2008, it was exactly what that room of discouraged salespeople needed.

Through his story, Michael told the salespeople that they were facing a similar choice. They could get in the pool and work, trusting that when times are hard there's an opportunity to get ahead, or they could get out.

"I watched that game from the stands, and it was the decision I regret most in my life. I know things are hard right now. I know that the pool's too cold, the practices too long, the rewards seem too far off. But this is our championship game. I refuse to quit until we win."

That keynote in July 2008 was a turning point both for Michael and the company. Instead of a hostile or disinterested crowd, he built a room of allies who rallied around a shared goal. His purpose story inspired his team. It gave them a reason to bring their best selves to work and to work toward the common goal to ride out the storm of recession and emerge stronger and better than ever. With no regrets.

The Purpose Story: A Components Breakdown

Once your message is clear and you search back through your career and life, using the hack above or one of your own to find a story that is perfectly suited to support it, your next job is to include the four components that make a story stick.

Identifiable Characters

More so than with any of the other essential stories—whose main characters are sometimes customers, as in the value story, or sometimes a stakeholder telling the founder story on behalf of the founder—the identifiable character in a purpose story is almost always the storyteller. The leader who learned the lesson. The person who had the experience. While you can tell a purpose story about someone else, the best ones are about yourself.

This is both exciting and challenging.

Exciting because the options for the stories you could tell are limited only by the number of days you remember being alive, and I mean that in a literal sense, not an existential one. As the identifiable character, it means any given moment in your life can become a purpose story if you match it to the right message. For example, one of my favorite purpose stories is one I heard when a speaker was uniting and inspiring the audience to follow their own purpose. He shared his experience of going through a bankruptcy and how he had to move in with his girlfriend. His office was a tiny desk squeezed in next to their bed. One night, his girlfriend came home, he was working at his tiny desk, and he had all of his bills and all of his paperwork from the bankruptcy laid out on the bed. She didn't want to disturb him, but it was late, so she walked in and kind of slid under the covers under all of his paperwork. He looked over at her, asleep under piles of paperwork, and thought, *This is the last time she has to sleep under the weight of my bills.* That moment became his fuel to never give up.

While you being the main identifiable character opens up unlimited purpose story material, as every Spider-Man knows, with great power comes great responsibility. Because though the main character is often the leader, the story is actually about the audience. Yes, Michael's water polo story was about him, but it was designed to prompt the audience to put themselves in his shoes. Yes, the CEO of the Maricopa Medical Center told a story about his first forum, but it was specifically designed and delivered so the audience would see themselves at that meeting and feel the same pride those present all shared.

The key to using identifiable characters well in a purpose story is to reveal details about yourself. Something as simple as what you were wearing that day or a specific observation you made or thought you had. But as you do, keep your audience in mind. What details will they relate to or connect with? What detail will make them say, "Yep—that's so me"?

Authentic Emotions

An effective way to blend the experience of the identifiable character (you, the leader) with the experience of the listener is to lean on emotions.

What makes a purpose story work is not how clearly you can recite the sequence of events. The success of your purpose story is dependent entirely on your ability and willingness to share how you felt about these events. These emotions don't have to be big. In fact, indifference is often the primary emotional state. What *does* need to be big—the bigger the better, really—is your willingness to be vulnerable, to share things about yourself that aren't typically shared in business.

Yes, you heard me. Vulnerability. My guess is you've heard this before, the importance of vulnerability in business leadership. And while it's not the most comfortable buzzword for business—no one wants to be exposed—research has shown time and time again that being vulnerable in business has the power to propel you to success.

Researcher, author, and famed vulnerability expert Brené Brown says, "Vulnerability is the absolute heartbeat of innovation and creativity. There can be zero innovation without vulnerability."[6] We all know that innovation and creativity are the things that will, ultimately, move business forward. But still we hesitate.

Part of the hesitation with being vulnerable in the workplace may stem from how people believe they will be perceived in those vulnerable moments. Brown says that sometimes people equate vulnerability with weakness,[7] but it's actually the opposite. Running a successful business means making yourself vulnerable to risk, ridicule, even failure as you take chances—chances on expanding the business, on making that big purchase.

Vulnerability also plays an important role when it comes to interacting with your employees. In her research, Brown found the root of social connection lies in vulnerability. When we're vulnerable in the workplace, we connect on a human level, increasing trust among leadership and employees, encouraging the sharing of ideas, and increasing loyalty.[8]

Fortunately, the purpose story is the perfect place to open up emotionally and get vulnerable. And you don't have to feel tied to telling a story from within the workplace. One of the most exciting freedoms of the purpose story is the opportunity to seek stories outside the walls of your company and the responsibilities of your role. Have a transformational moment while at sleepaway camp? Fair game. Learn an important lesson from the fallout of a friendship? A viable option. Not only does this give you endless purpose story material, choosing stories beyond the office gives your team the chance to connect with you as a human, not just as a corporate figure, which, unless you actually are a robot, is a very good thing.

A Moment

Like the previous two story types, your purpose story will be more compelling if it includes a specific moment in time. This can be accomplished by including something as specific as a place or a time the audience can picture, like sitting in the bleachers watching a water polo game.

I find, with purpose stories in particular, the moment often coincides with the explosion. It's the split second before a realization. It's the crossover point between the normal, where things had been moving along as they usually do, and the moment when things suddenly change. You learn a lesson. You gain a new perspective. You enter the new normal.

That being said, although the moment may occur in a split second in real life, in the story it should feel a little bit like slow motion. Where you zoom way in and take your time.

For example, I hosted a workshop at an offsite retreat for a group of executives. They were working on a variety of story types, and one was a purpose story about finding a balance in work and life. A woman shared a story of realizing how much time she was missing with her kids. But she didn't just say, "I realized how much time I was missing with my kids." Instead, she expertly included the moment component by painting the exact picture of the realization: "I'll never forget it. I was in my car, hands on the steering wheel, driving down the freeway, thirty minutes into my one-hour commute, and I realized, this drive has stolen too many hours from me and my family." When her story was done and the group debriefed what worked about the story, everyone agreed that moment in the car stood out and drew them in.

Specific Details

The success of a purpose story hinges on the leader's ability to make a story that is technically about him or her feel like a story that's about the audience. With that in mind, whenever possible, build in audience universal truths. Details, situations, emotions you know the majority of your audience is familiar with. The vice president of the tech company knew that many of the people in his audience had or have had teenagers in their home. If they were not a parent, everyone in the room had been a teenager at some point and could relate. In Michael's story, he knew the room had stood at the crossroads of wanting to quit; in fact, many of them were standing there at that moment as he was talking. I've used details as specific as the My Little Pony dream castle in one of my stories, knowing my audience had been raised in the eighties and nineties and would remember the cherished toy. I once used the shoe brand Mootsie Tootsie, knowing that a particular audience would be mostly Gen Y females.

In each instance, the use of specific details helps blur the lines between the identifiable character (the leader) and the audience until they become one and the same. And in that moment, your purpose becomes their purpose.

Purpose Stories and the Last
Company Culture Frontier

In 2010, a psychologist at Emory University set out to determine what made emotionally healthy, happy kids and administered a test to elementary students in an effort to reveal some insight.[9] The test was comprised of twenty simple yes-or-no questions designed to measure how much of their family history each student knew.

Do you know where your grandparents grew up?

Do you know where your mom and dad went to high school?

Do you know where your parents met?

Do you know an illness or something really terrible that happened in your family?

Do you know the story of your birth?

The results of the study were astonishing. The more the child knew about their family's history, the stronger their sense of control over their lives and the higher their self-esteem. The "Do You Know?" scale turned out to be the best single predictor of children's emotional health and happiness.

Our team couldn't help but wonder if the same could be true for organizations. Was it possible the more team members knew about their leaders and the stories of the company, the more connected they would feel to the organization as a whole? So we tested it.

We administered a national survey to one thousand full-time US employees ranging from eighteen years old to sixty-five years old to see what they knew about their company's stories and, for those who did know stories about their company, if that made a difference in their overall job satisfaction. For example, the survey asked questions like the following:

Do you know the story of how the company you work for started/came to be?

Do you know if the company you work for has ever faced challenges or setbacks in its history?

Our results revealed that those participants who answered yes to those two questions were 40 percent more likely to affirm "the work we do at the company makes a difference in the world."

A little storytelling can go a long way in driving purpose in a company, and that sense of purpose is what leads to lasting success. The purpose story helps your team understand that what they do matters. There's a chance the woman writing code at her bedroom desk three time zones away doesn't know she's an important piece to what you're all trying to do, and the guy at the desk three cubicles away probably doesn't either. None of them may realize they're part of something bigger, something important, something with a powerful *why*. And they need to.

It's easy to think of customers and investors as the only people you need to sell to. They're the ones whose attention you need to grab, who you need to influence, who you need to transform. But as a leader, you're facing the exact same job with your people. If you can't engage them and influence them, you can't do much of anything except write checks and hope people do enough to justify them.

It's a daily battle. One that, if you're not already fighting it, you're losing.

The question is, are you telling the right stories?

We'd like to believe that it's open floor plans or employee manuals or staff basketball courts or kombucha and beer on tap that establishes a company culture, because then all we'd have to do is a little remodeling and keg installation and we'd be set. But it is actually the intentional and painstaking commitment to storytelling that builds and sustains culture.

Culture is a collection of stories that align and inspire. Employees feel more connected and happier when they know about the history of their company. The ups, the downs, and where it all started. More importantly, when they know how the company faced adversity and lived to tell about it, they know the company can weather the storm.

These stories—this sense of history—are the same for employees as it is for families who tell their origin stories to their kids. Knowing their culture gives employees a sense of belonging.

Get your stories right, and you're golden. Get your stories wrong, and the bridges to maintaining your people are as wobbly as the ones that permeate children's playgrounds and make your footing feel unsure and your grounding shaky.

Does your team know how the company was founded? The biggest account landed? The biggest failures? The greatest trials and triumphs, catastrophes and comebacks?

When the day-to-day of coming to work becomes tedious, when your team misses a goal, when your organization faces adversity (which it will), do your people know they are a part of something bigger?

If you tell your stories, they will.

In Sickness and In Health

When times are good, a purpose story can drive a business to better performance through better culture. When times are tough, like they were for Michael's company, it can mean nothing short of survival. Regardless of the times, a purpose story is one anyone can tell—especially you. And often.

Of course, that is not true for all stories. There are some stories you cannot tell. That's what the next chapter is about.

CHAPTER SEVEN

The Customer Story

Sweet-Smelling Armpits and the Story You Can't Tell

Branding is what people say about you when you're not in the room.

—JEFF BEZOS

They say public speaking is one of the world's greatest fears. And while I suspect that old tale is a little overblown, it's certainly not uncommon to feel some anxiety before taking the podium. That's true even for professional speakers; it just goes with the territory.

My top-notch professional secret? Use great deodorant.

Okay, that's not really my best public speaking advice. But if your goal were to create a really lousy deodorant commercial, I think that advice might be your starting point.

Cue the cheesy announcer.

Kindra Hall is a professional storyteller. And when the story gets tough, she counts on her deodorant to get her through to the end. It's why she chooses Acme, the brand most trusted by story experts around the world.

Meh.

This kind of marketing makes me nuts for many reasons. One is it just sounds cheesy. To be fair to Acme, this issue is a tricky one; as long as the messenger is you, you run the risk of coming across as fake or inauthentic.

But more than that, these kinds of messages drive me crazy because they reek of missed opportunity. There is a story there, but Acme just didn't put in the effort to tell a good one.

Fortunately, there's a solution for dealing with this problem that's just about as old as commerce itself. To understand it, let's look at a real-world counterpart of our fictional Acme example.

My experience with Native Deodorant began like most online shopping experiences. I made my purchase, filed away my email receipt, and received the product. Fairly typical. But what wasn't typical was what a great job of marketing Native does. Their value proposition—deodorant that is safe, effective, and made in the USA—is clear and easy to grasp, and they've put it front and center. You need approximately three seconds on the Native website to know exactly what problem they're solving.

Where Native truly excels, however, is in the use of a unique story, namely, their ability to capture stories from people like me *after* they've used the product. Arguably the most challenging of the four story types, Native is on its way to mastering the elusive but oh-so-powerful customer story.

The Customer Story

You already know the customer story well. You've seen its echoes in things like testimonials, reviews, influencer endorsements, referrals, and recommendations. The long history of customers praising (or panning) products is a pastime that just keeps on giving.

Customer experiences have a natural edge over traditional marketing because they come preloaded with what the Acme story lacks: credibility. When you tell someone your product is great, that's called marketing. When another customer tells them, it's called a referral, and referrals carry a whole different level of clout. Studies consistently show that reviews and referrals have an enormous influence on customer behavior. The power of social media and review sites like Yelp and Angie's List make leaving—and reading—reviews easier than ever. Consider these findings from a BrightLocal consumer review survey:

- 85 percent of consumers trust online reviews as much as personal recommendations.
- Positive reviews make 73 percent of consumers trust a local business more.
- 49 percent of consumers need to see at least a four-star rating before they choose to use a business.
- Consumers read an average of seven reviews before trusting a business.[1]

But while consumers are seeking out and reading reviews, research also shows that consumers are often skeptical and on the lookout for fake testimonials.

A 2016 Pew Research Study found "business owners and consumers alike have voiced concerns about the validity and truthfulness of the information posted on various online review sites. And when asked about this issue, Americans themselves are nearly evenly split. Roughly half (51 percent) of those who read online reviews say they generally give an accurate picture of the true quality of the product, but a similar share (48 percent) believes it is often hard to tell if online reviews are truthful and unbiased."[2]

This is where customer stories can help.

While referrals, reviews, testimonials, or other shared customer experiences can be valuable, they don't necessarily come packaged as a story, and as a result, they don't have the same impact a story can have. A review might answer questions, but it rarely includes the normal—that first part of the story framework—or draws people in with specific details that inspire imagery in the mind of the reader. A testimonial might state the facts, but rarely does it include compelling emotions. A product review might be good for business, but turning it into a customer story is great for business. A customer story draws people in, makes them care, feel connected, and perhaps most importantly, makes them feel understood; for example, "Someone else, like me, has felt the way I've felt and wanted the thing I've wanted and found the solution here. I want that. I'll buy it."

Yes. A well-told customer story can make all of that happen.

Switching Storytellers: Customer Story Versus Value Story

Now, I will admit, there is a chance you are thinking this is a value story. Isn't this just a story to describe the value of the product? Is this a chapter I can skip?

The answer is no. No, you cannot skip this chapter.

I mean you can, but while value stories and customer stories are different means to the same end, the difference between them is something you don't want to miss. Unless, of course, you're okay with your competition figuring it out and having a leg up on you. In that case, go ahead. Skip all the chapters you want.

Recall value stories use the Steller storytelling framework to reveal the value of the product. Good sales and marketing are often a value story job. The identifiable character is the customer living in their own normal and having a problem. Along comes the explosion (the product or service) and, voilà! the problem is solved.

Normal → Explosion → New Normal

When Unbounce told the story of the marketer struggling to create and test new online content while dealing with the bottleneck of budgets and developers, they were talking about a customer. When Workiva told the story of the aspiring triathlete who realized his dream because of the time saved using their product, they were talking about a customer. And while all of these stories were about customers, they were value stories.

A customer story is different.

A customer story has a unique twist.

A customer story, while it might illustrate value, is told by the customer him or herself. Check out the Native website and you'll see it. Stories illustrating value but told by customers. Try this five-star wonder from Amy H.:[3]

Eliminates Stink Completely

Breast cancer runs in my family, so I started trying natural deodorants to lower my risk. One particular "like" product with similar ingredients left chemical burns on my underarms. It was 4.00 cheaper. I tried others, but they don't work past walking out my front door. I live in the south so it's humid and hot. I sweat a lot and I was nervous about giving up antiperspirant. I reluctantly ordered Native because it was so pricey in comparison. I'm 100% glad I ordered it. It truly doesn't take much and it works in the hot and humid south. No stink all day!!! Now if I could slather my dogs in this stuff my world would be stink free. :-)

And this little ditty from Carolyn D.:[4]

Active Grandmother

My granddaughter left hers on my bathroom counter and I decided to try it. I have tried so many brands in my seventy-seven years that I was truly amazed that I no longer had an odor after biking or or paddleboarding. I am just now placing my first order of the coconut/vanilla. Can't wait!

At first blush, these could be perceived as value stories: customers with problems whose problems are solved. But there's one key element that make these customer stories: the people telling them.

If these were true value stories, we might have the same character (Amy H. or Carolyn D.) and the same explosion/product (Native Deodorant). We'd have the same outcome. The same value. The difference is that Amy and Carolyn are telling the stories—not Native. And that difference makes all the difference.

If, like Acme, Native told the story themselves, it would go something like this:

Amy H. had breast cancer in her family and was trying to reduce the risk associated with conventional deodorants. Every natural solution she tried either left her with chemical burns or didn't hold up in the humid weather of the South. Native saved the day!

Carolyn D. borrowed her granddaughter's bar of Native and was truly amazed that after seventy-seven years of trying different brands, she no longer had odor after biking or paddleboarding.

Either one of those statements could be transformed into a value story. Add a little more emotion, build out the normal, and with some tweaking and work, we could turn that into a great video ad, some online copy, or even a dramatic poster or billboard. But even with those adjustments, we wouldn't be tapping into the critical leverage point that a customer story has and a value story lacks: inherent credibility.

Why Customer Stories Are More Credible

The customer story is in a world of its own because it eliminates the nagging voice that questions whether or not you can believe a story if it's the seller telling it. With a customer story, it's not the company, it's a person—just like you—who tried it and loved it and has nothing to gain by telling you.

As consumers, we're far more sophisticated than we used to be. We have far more power and information in the marketplace than ever before. And that's made us, if not suspicious, then at least cautious when it comes to what businesses tell us. And that includes stories. Used properly, the customer story solves any remaining doubt. The Amy H. and Carolyn D. examples show us why.

The Source Matters

Think about it for a minute. What if Native were to say their product "eliminates stink completely," like they made that a part of their marketing vernacular, even sharing it in a value story. There is something different about hearing it from an actual customer; it simply means more coming from Amy. Or there's the bit about the high price tag. Native saying they're worth the additional expense feels like a justification, but Amy saying it feels like a fact.

I know, it may seem that what we're really talking about here is something you likely discussed in third grade during the twenty minutes dedicated to creative writing. First person versus third person. I and me versus she and he. And you would be right. But it turns out, sometimes the source is the thing that matters most.

McDonald's learned this the hard way in the United Kingdom.

In 2017, they released a commercial that started with a boy smack dab in the middle of that awkward preteen phase and sitting on a bed.

He's sifting through what appears to be a box of junk, but we quickly realize the items in the box are in fact precious keepsakes. A pair of eyeglasses. A wristwatch. A handwritten note. All physical memories.

After examining the box, the boy asks his mother, "What was Dad like?"

The mother looks at him and then takes him on a walk and starts to tell him about his father's best traits. As they pass an old stone church, she tells her son his father was as big as a building. The young man stands a little taller, attempting to look bigger. When they walk by a soccer game, she details how his father was not only a great soccer player but captain of the team. The boy awkwardly tries to kick a ball back onto the pitch, but he's clearly not soccer captain material. When they sit on a bench, the mother talks about the boy's father being a smart dresser, with shoes so shiny you could see your reflection in them. The boy looks at his scruffy sneakers. Discouragement is written all over his face.

Their walk ends as they sit down to eat at McDonald's. The boy opens his kid's meal, pulls out a fish sandwich, and takes a big bite. As he starts to chew, the camera pans to the mother, who remarks in a wistful tone that the fish sandwich was his father's favorite sandwich and he never ate one without getting tartar sauce all over his chin. Her voice cracks as she sees her handsome son with a spot of sauce on his face.

The boy is thrilled. Finally. A similarity.

Outrage over the ad was intense and widespread. I read about it in the *New York Times* over a cup of coffee. How dare they exploit child bereavement! Who needs two parents when you have Filet-O-Fish?! The ad was pulled shortly after it aired, and McDonald's issued an apology.

Although I had not seen the ad before reading the article, I had two distinct thoughts. The first was of my own father and tomato juice.

When I was in college, I was on a flight with my mother. The flight attendant asked for our beverage order and I requested tomato juice. My mom looked at me abruptly.

"What?!" I responded. "I didn't order a Bloody Mary. I just asked for tomato juice." (It's amazing how quickly we can revert to our teenage selves when we're with our mothers.)

"No," she said. "It's not that. It's just that your dad always orders tomato juice when he flies. He doesn't drink it anywhere else, only on planes."

I've never forgotten the deep sense of pride I felt in that moment. Yes, it was about something as simple as tomato juice, but I still feel the unique sense of daughterly joy and connection to my dad I felt in that moment.

At this point, you might suspect that my father passed away when I was a child. Which is why something like tomato juice can mean so much to me. But that's not true. My father is very much alive, and I talk with him often. And yet his aliveness didn't in any way dilute how meaningful it was to know an instance of how we are similar. So I could see how a boy who *had* lost his father might cherish that connection, even if it was over a fast-food sandwich.

A freelance journalist for *The Guardian* echoed this sentiment, although from a different experience. Her mother had passed in 1985 when the writer was young. She said, "I am still eager for crumbs of information about my mother. . . . Unearthing a new fact, or hearing an observation about our similarities from someone who knew her, feels like a wonderful kind of archaeology."[5]

That was my first thought: my dad, tomato juice, and how much pride I took in knowing we were alike in that way.

My second thought: I wonder if that McDonald's ad was a real story? Was there really a boy who discovered this random similarity with a father he lost, and somehow McDonald's UK heard about it?

Maybe his mom told them the story, and the ad agency was touched by it and realized they had stumbled upon marketing gold and decided they would tell that story! It would have identifiable characters and emotions (of course, they wouldn't call it that, because our research hadn't been completed yet, but you get the point). Then they wrote the storyboard and cast the characters, and even though the whole thing was a true story . . .

They told it as a value story rather than having the boy tell it himself, as a customer story. They ruined it without knowing how or why.

Yes, the source matters, for better or worse.

The Details Matter

As the saying goes, you can't make this stuff up. Carolyn D.'s customer story is filled with tiny details that help the story ring true. Her teenage granddaughter leaving the deodorant out on the bathroom counter (typical teenager), the specific activities Carolyn enjoys (bicycling, paddleboarding). Even her age was specific: seventy-seven. And did you notice something else? In her review, Carolyn duplicated the word *or*. A small thing, but an important one.

When it comes to customer stories, stories coming straight from the source, the ring of truth is critically important. While it may be tempting, whether in print or video, to airbrush your customer stories, sometimes the giggles, the bloopers, and the imperfections are what make them more real. Certainly, you should guide the stories to fit the framework and include the necessary components. And if the aggrievances are big, spare your customer any embarrassment. But don't edit them beyond recognition. The beauty of a customer story is its raw, imperfect realness.

You can put a hundred copywriters in a room for a week, and nothing they write will make us believe that a real person exists behind the words as well as Carolyn does. Her details fill out the story and make it more believable, but they also do double duty by informing others about the kind of person who uses Native. They are adventurous, vibrant, and full of life, no matter their age.

The devil may be in the details, but so is the delight and so is the credibility.

Going Native: How to Get
the Customer Story

Yes, collecting reviews is old news. Amazon's been doing it forever, and companies were doing it for a century before that. But Native does it better, and you can too. Here are two simple rules for following their lead and curating customer stories of your own.

Rule 1: You Must Ask

A few days after my deodorant arrived, I received an email from Native:

> To: Kindra Hall
> Subject: Thanks for your support, Kindra!
>
> Hey Kindra,
>
> Hope you are doing well! I wanted to thank you for supporting Native Deodorant. We're a small, family-owned business and genuinely appreciate it. :)
>
> Since you've had a few days to try Native Deodorant, I'd love to get your initial thoughts on the product. In particular, I'd love to know what deodorant you were using prior to switching to Native, and what made you willing to try Native? Have you enjoyed your experience with Native so far? If you've had a great experience with Native, we'd really appreciate it if you could post a review of our deodorant here!
>
> Any feedback would be greatly appreciated. If you have any questions, please don't hesitate to email me.
>
> Have a fantastic day!
>
> Best,
> Julia
>
> P.S. We'll send you a free bar of Native if you send us a video of you reviewing it! Find out more here.

This email is doing some surprising things (more on that below), but its most important job right now is to get me to write a review. It's a prompt, a request to tell my customer story to Native. A request that has yielded 7,008 responses thus far and counting and now is the center of a TV ad for their product.

This may seem simple, but few companies do it. And it illustrates the most critical first rule of the customer story: if you want customer stories, you must ask for them. Sure, you might get the occasional unprompted letter, but it'll take you years to curate a body of customer stories if you don't ask.

Asking is not hard. You just need a system. A follow-up email like the one Native uses is a super easy system that gets the job done.

Notice, though, that Native takes asking to a new level.

- The email arrives after the product. Anyone can throw an "Add your review here!" link on an emailed invoice. But that's not much help when you haven't yet received the product. Your ask needs to come after the customer has experienced your product or service.
- The email is from a real human with a real name: Julia. She's friendly. She lets me know I'm important to their family-owned company. And I'll be darned if she doesn't seem completely authentic to me. Unlike an automated, faceless chatbot, robo-thing. If I reply to Julia, I'll get a response.
- I can get a gift. If I create a video review, they'll send me a free bar of deodorant. There's nothing like thank-yous and free stuff to get people to respond. And if I film my own video, they avoid the possibility of a McDonald's debacle completely.

Asking is a skill. But it starts with just asking. Don't make it harder than it needs to be. Start asking and tweak as you go.

Rule 2: Ask Specifically and You Shall Receive

Beyond the simple act of asking, the Native email sets the stage for ensuring another critical piece of the puzzle: guiding my response so I share an actual story.

This is about story, after all. We don't just want stars or thumbs-up or basic praise. We want stories because they work a whole lot better.

Julia's email specifically asks what I was using before I tried Native and how things are now that I've been using it for a few days. Notice anything? They're giving me a framework to deliver a story to them. That framework, lo and behold, just happens to match up perfectly with our framework. By asking for comments in this way, Julia is guiding my response so, if I follow her directions, my comments will come back in the shape of a perfect normal–explosion–new normal story with Native Deodorant as the explosion in the middle.

And in case I forgot to respond in that manner, these prompts were reinforced once I went to the review page. There I was subtly prompted again to shape my review in the form of an effective story.

It is guidance like this that likely led to the multitude of high-quality stories on the website. Guidance that encouraged Amy to tell the whole story. It's what encouraged Carolyn to include the part about finding it on her bathroom counter and trying her granddaughter's deodorant, which, if you think about it, is a little rebellious and makes the whole thing even cooler and more real. When seeking customer stories, ask the questions that will elicit the kind of responses you're looking for.

Customer stories are quite possibly the easiest and most powerful type of story to use. If you have customers, you have stories. You just have to find them. Instead of building them from scratch yourself, your job is simply to curate and tell them.

If a Customer Story Falls in the Woods but Nobody Tells It . . .

Of course, stories aren't worth much if they aren't told. Think of your job here as that of chief curator. You've collected the exhibits for your customer story museum, but they won't work for you if you don't put them on display.

The question of course is where? Where are these stories?

For the answer to that, I think back to my childhood mornings before school.

Wake up. Go to the kitchen. Get a box of cereal. Pour some cereal into a bowl with some milk. Then eat the cereal while staring at the back of the cereal box. Did you ever do that? Oh, man, the number of hours I spent reading the exact same cereal box. I read the random facts and tried to solve the puzzles while shoveling sugary puffs of something into my mouth (yes, I grew up in the eighties and we ate sugary puffed things back then).

Although my kids don't eat cereal now, the memory of those mornings got me thinking. What if the cereal company had printed a story on that box? They would have had at least twenty-five minutes of my undivided attention—undivided because what else was I gonna look at while I ate breakfast?

Now, I'm not saying print your customer stories on cereal boxes (although you could), but, instead, think about those empty spaces in your customers' lives. Spaces that you know they fill with something. Now that you know they prefer story, why not put a story there? From websites and newsletters to video and keynote speeches. Trade show booths to bids and proposals. Sales calls to team meetings. The walls of a subway car.

For Native, their customer story museum is their website. For a hotel in Canada where I stayed once, there was a journal in the room for guests to write the story of their experience: why they were there, what they did, what they loved about their stay. This was their customer story space. Social media is another obvious place to display customer stories. Essentially, any place your customers go and have room in their minds, tell a story there.

The Customer Story: A Components Breakdown

Did you notice something while reading this chapter? You're starting to speak fluent storytelling? It's true. We've been talking in terms of identifiable characters, authentic emotions, moments, and specific details throughout the customer story discussion because, let's face it, a story can't be separated from the sum of its component parts.

But, by default, you have less control of this story (because it's not yours, it's theirs), so a deep understanding of the components is key to helping a customer story achieve its full potential. Here's the full scoop on how to use the four components to maximize your customers' stories.

Identifiable Characters

Get ready for some earth-shattering news. The identifiable character in a customer story is *the customer*. I know. Crazy. When it comes to the identifiable character in a customer story, it's much less about the who and more about the how. How do you enable the customer to be a character your audience can relate to and trust? The answer varies depending on the means by which you are sharing your story.

If, like Native Deodorant, you are building a story museum based on customer reviews, make sure the process you use and the questions you ask encourage customers to express their true selves. Thumbs up versus thumbs down gives very little insight into the people who own these thumbs.

If you want to take a more active approach to your customer stories—perhaps catch them on video, post an image and story on Instagram, or maybe have them share their story onstage at a live event—and you have identified a few customers who are up for the challenge, then remember this: perfection is your enemy. Too smooth is suspicious.

I watched the bonus commentary on the 2003 movie *Love Actually*, and I'll never forget what the director said during the final scene when the elementary-school-aged girl belted out the classic Christmas anthem "All I Want for Christmas." Apparently, she was too good to be believable. They had to ask her to sing it again, but not so perfectly. They needed scratches in the record in order for the character to be believable.

The fact that a child singer can be that good is a conversation for another time. For now, when it comes to your identifiable character, resist the urge to make the character perfect, the urge to smooth any rough edges. Movies and commercials need actors; customer stories just need customers.

Authentic Emotions

The great advantage of customer stories and why your extra effort to seek them out is worth it is that authentic emotion lives in every word. There is nothing more authentic than what naturally flows from a customer whose life has been changed by what you offer. But more valuable than the emotions they felt after experiencing your product or service are the emotions they felt before. Customer stories live and die based on the emotions that are shared in the normal of the story.

When seeking and telling customer stories, remember this: the joy or relief they felt (authentic emotion) after finding you only matters when placed in contrast to how they felt *before* finding you.

A Moment

Like the previous story types, including a specific moment strengthens the effectiveness of a customer story. And while your control over these stories has its limitations, you can encourage the inclusion of a moment by asking questions like "Where were you the first time you tried our product?" or "Do you remember where you were when you first heard about our service?" These questions are moment-driven. The answer you receive will often include the moment *for* you.

Specific Details

As mentioned earlier, the specific details are what give the customer story its irresistible ring of truth. The offhanded comments or specks of reality so small they risk being written off completely. Of course, you would never do that; you now know better.

This is perhaps the most rewarding, fun component of customer stories: hearing the unique details of your customers' experiences that you otherwise wouldn't know. I don't think I will ever tire of reading emails that describe how my customers (typically people in the audience of my keynotes or who read my work) have used their stories. They include details like what hors d'oeuvres were served at the networking hour as they shared a story with a new contact or the sound of the CEO impatiently clicking his pen before a big presentation—a clicking that stopped once my customer told a story.

Keep your ears out for these little details and pay attention to your own imagination when they tell you or write you with their story. What details engaged your co-creative response? What details did your subconscious pick up on and run with? Let that be your guide for the details that ultimately get shared.

One Last Truth About Customer Stories

Before we wrap up this chapter and move to the final part of the book, let me take off my rose-colored glasses for a moment and say out loud what you may be thinking after reading this chapter.

Customer stories aren't easy.

I was working with an international brand who wanted to tell the story of one of their customers. But when it came time to discuss which customer's story we should tell, the team immediately suggested we create a customer versus actually find one. Create a persona and then hire an actor to play the part. They felt this would be an easier path—which is true! It takes extra work to find customers, talk with them, ask what their story really is. It's time consuming to listen and ask questions that allow you to reveal the authentic emotion and specific details. In many cases the marketing team, who are often the ones tasked with telling the story, have absolutely no interaction with customers. This isn't a criticism; it's a reality. Their job is to sit in boardrooms with whiteboard walls and create customers, and meanwhile, at the reception desk or sitting in the customer service call center are the people who actually interact with customers.

The customer story can be challenging simply because you have less control over the story by default—it's not yours, it's theirs. But I find the real challenge with the customer story is a symptom of a much bigger issue in business: namely, how acceptable it has become to be disconnected from our actual customers. Customer communications has become siloed and automated and, as a result, has created a story wasteland. With no real customer conversations, we're left to make up versions of them based on data and surveys.

So, yes, the customer story requires a few extra steps and effort, but imagine how transformative it would be if you encouraged your team and committed yourself to seek out customer stories and allowed your customers' true voices to be heard.

Creating Your Own Essential Stories

We've reached the end of part 2 and the four essential stories that businesses need in order to thrive. In part 3, we'll take a step-by-step look at how you can do three very specific things:

- Find the potential stories within your business by choosing what story type serves you best and then collecting possible stories to tell.
- Craft the best ideas into great stories using the Steller storytelling framework and some tried-and-true techniques to make the job as easy as possible.
- Tell your own essential business stories in an authentic way that will help you bridge the gap to audiences of all types and make your stories stick.

As storytellers like to say, "And now the plot thickens!" Let's get to it.

PART THREE

Create Your Story

Finding, Crafting, and

Telling Your Story

CHAPTER EIGHT

Finding Your Story

How to Find Stories Anywhere

To be a person is to have a story to tell.
—Isak Dinesen

In October 2006, I was invited to speak at the Mesa Storytelling Festival in Mesa, Arizona. The festival was known for bringing in the best tellers of the time, and I was excited beyond description, not only for the opportunity to tell a story to an eager and engaged audience, but also because I would have the honor of introducing the star performer of the whole event. My mentor. My idol. Donald Davis.

I sat next to him, right before his set, as another teller performed on stage. I shifted in my seat, fiddled my fingers, shook my leg violently, all to release the nerves I felt about introducing the most important man in my life besides my father (Michael and I were newly dating at the time and he was definitely behind Donald).

In perfect contrast to my demeanor, Donald was calm, cool, and loosely holding a worn piece of paper. I wondered if that paper detailed stage-fright strategies, so I strained to read what was on it. From over his shoulder I saw a list of words written in handwriting I knew to be his. Names of people. Notations of situations or happenings or moments. Four or five columns of them, each with at least twenty words. I remember thinking the words on the paper slightly resembled the way the episodes were listed on my collection of *Friends* DVDs: "The One with Joey's New Brain" or "The One Where Chandler Doesn't Like Dogs."

And then I recognized them for what they really were: possible stories. In his hand Donald was holding a list of hundreds of possible stories he could tell in his set. I leaned in slightly, visually eavesdropping on the list. So many stories.

My spying was cut short by the sound of applause. The teller on the stage had finished, and I was up. I took the stage, grabbed the microphone, and I did my best to do him justice. As I said his name, I watched Donald decisively fold up the list of story options, place it in his pocket, straighten his bowtie, and walk to the stage. I spent the next ninety minutes listening, in awe, to the stories he decided to tell. I couldn't help but wonder when I would get to hear the rest of the stories he didn't tell from that list.

The single biggest barrier to not telling your story isn't procrastination or being afraid of sharing or stage fright; it's assuming you don't have a story in the first place.

─────

This is originally what kept me from telling my stories. It was the early 2000s when I first felt the desire to tell stories from my own life. But I hesitated. What right did I have—a young twentysomething from a loving, middle-class home—to share my stories? They weren't painful enough. They weren't dark enough. I should keep them to myself. It wasn't until I took a chance at an open mic night in Oklahoma City, where I shared a story of your run-of-the-mill heartbreak, that I realized people connect with stories no matter how big or tragic or small and sweet they are, as long as they are real.

Even if your stories are small, you have them, and they are worth telling.

That being said, no one is immune to this fear of storylessness. Even people with big stories think they don't have them. I'll never forget when I took a seat on an airplane and glanced at the gentleman seated next to me. He was a smallish, unassuming man, mousy brown hair, glasses, and in his midfifties. As I sat down, he barely looked up. He was engrossed in a phone conversation and staring at a tablet device with a very, very furrowed brow. As I slid into my seat I overheard pieces of his conversation, which prompted me to, not unlike at that storytelling festival with Donald Davis, glimpse at his screen and the photo of a massive fire that, if my eyes weren't deceiving me, was coming out of the ground.

The man zoomed in and out of the image of the fire, an image that— once I realized my seatmate was far too wrapped up in his conversation to pay any attention to whether or not I was looking—showed a man with a shield trying to approach the fire.

My seatmate mumbled something about concrete shrapnel on the ground, that the rig had been compromised, and that, yes, he was going to have to turn around and head back to the Middle East. He ended the call, then immediately called someone else and told them to pack for seven weeks and catch the earliest flight to the Middle East.

He ended that call and sighed.

Uncomfortable with the sudden silence, I decided to fill the space with some awkward airplane talk and nervously laughed about overhead bin space. We exchanged the standard airplane platitudes until he revealed he was supposed to be visiting his mother for her ninetieth birthday.

"But it sounds like I'm going to have to turn around and head back to the Middle East."

I responded with my best feign of innocence, "Oh?"

He revealed he was an international expert in fighting oil-rig fires once they've been attacked by terrorists. He was quiet and reserved as he told me about his work, about his best friend who died in the oil field when he inhaled a deadly gas, and how, although his grown children and wife wished he would retire, he still felt compelled to train others to fight these fires.

I was totally captivated by his story for the entire flight. As we began our descent, I asked him if he ever shared these stories.

He looked at me in disbelief.

"Stories? I don't have any stories," he said, seriously.

And though his stories were riveting without effort, what struck me more—what always strikes me—was that he didn't see them as stories. Or at least not stories worth telling.

If you've ever let the belief you don't have a story stop you from telling one, let me assure you, you are profoundly wrong. Yes, stories come in all shapes and sizes, but each of us has them and there is a place for all of them.

The problem isn't that you don't have them.

It's that you don't know how to find them.

Fortunately, that is a problem we can fix.

Finding Stories in Two Steps

By this point, you should be convinced of the power of story. You know why story is so important, how it works, and the four essential story types for business. But the doubt may still linger. *Do I even have a story to tell? If I do, how do I find the right one?* These are the two burning questions we are going to answer next, and to do that, I'm going to break the answer into two distinct processes: collecting and choosing.

The first process is *story collection*. Story collection is about generating story ideas without regard for whether they're any good or appropriate or useful or even tellable. Story collection is good old-fashioned brainstorming, but with a few tools to help you avoid the intimidation of the blank page.

The second process is *story choosing*. Not all stories will work for all situations. I once had to give a speech at my high school National Honor Society banquet and, after procrastinating until the last minute, decided to tell a story about a clogged drain. Don't ask. But, yes, it was as ill-received as you might think. I learned the hard way that finding a story is one thing; choosing the right story is another.

Good story finding is a combination of both collecting and choosing.

Finding the Story, Phase 1: Story Collecting

Have you ever tried to get a story from an elderly relative? I once asked my grandmother about the Great Depression. I needed to write a paper for a school project. I sat down with her, paper and pen in hand, tape recorder ready to capture every last detail of the stories she would no doubt unleash on me.

I asked her, "Grandma, tell me about the Great Depression." Then I braced myself, pen ready.

"Oh, I don't know," she mused. "It was good."

And that was it. That was all she had to say.

I remember staring at her. After all, that was the opposite of everything I'd heard about the Great Depression. Depression was in the title, for heaven's sake. It wasn't the Great Good. Not only was I immediately concerned for my grade on the paper, I was also super disappointed and frustrated. I knew my grandma was full of stories. Why wouldn't she tell them to me?

From my years of working with leaders in the area of strategic storytelling, I know this is likely where you will get stuck and you won't know why. You'll know you need a story, and you'll ask yourself, "What story should I tell? What story should I tell?" And the responses you'll get from yourself will be much like the response my grandmother gave to me. Nothing. And you'll be just as discouraged as I was.

But it wasn't that my grandmother didn't have any stories, and it wasn't my grandmother's fault she didn't unleash a deluge of stories upon me. It isn't a lack of stories that keeps you from being able to find yours but rather the ineffective questions we use to get them. I asked my grandma a bad question. Getting better stories, or stories in the first place, requires asking better questions. And when it comes to better questions, there's one very important thing to remember: our stories attach themselves to the nouns in our lives.

The nouns in our lives are the people, the places, the things, the events in our lives.

When you are struggling to find a story, one key to a better question is to shift your thinking to nouns. Make a list of people or places or things or events. And as you write each one down, allow some mental space for the memories connected to those nouns to come to you.

For example, several years ago I spent an afternoon with my grandfather, who had just celebrated his ninety-third birthday. Since I don't often see him and rarely one-on-one, I was eager to hear some of his stories, particularly from his experience in World War II. So instead of saying, "Grandpa, tell me about World War II," I focused my question on a noun.

"Grandpa," I asked, "where were you stationed in World War II?"

He said Perth, Australia.

"Grandpa," I said, "Tell me about Perth, Australia."

It was as if I had said the secret word that opened a hidden cave of stories. For an hour and a half, my grandfather told me, in great detail, about his experience in Perth, a.k.a. stories about his World War II experiences. He told me about the barracks they slept in. How the rats ran across the top bunks all night long. He told me about a boarded-up town and the adventures they would take on the weekends, heading up the coast. All because I switched the question to focus on a place instead of a general experience.

This shift, of course, works for all kinds of story-seeking endeavors, including those in business. Particularly if you are often tasked with delivering purpose stories to align teams. Using the noun approach to find stories gives you endless access to story possibilities.

People, Places, Things, Stories

Several years ago I worked with an executive who needed to create a message about innovation. The message needed to communicate the difficult reality that, while innovation is amazing, it can also be painful at times. The message was a timely one, and it was important to him that he didn't just talk about innovation but rather tell a story about it, and hope, when they found themselves in one of those painful moments, his audience would likely remember this message and thereby be more adept at handling the pain.

Unfortunately, much like asking my grandmother about the Great Depression, searching for stories without a strategic approach wasn't yielding any results. So we decided to focus on nouns to help dig up some options. We made lists of the various technological object innovations he had witnessed in his lifetime with the hope that, by listing them, a story might emerge.

We made a list of music players he'd seen in his life: record players, eight-track players, boomboxes, Walkman, Discman, and iPods.

Then we made a list of the various computers he'd had or seen or used.

Then we made a list of the various phones in his life: rotary phone, cordless phones, and cell phones.

With each noun we would briefly chat about any memories that came up—memories that could, with a little crafting work, become a story. And while there were bits of stories that could be told for any of the nouns, it wasn't until we got to cell phones that a perfect story jumped out at us.

In the process of listing the phones, the man remembered the first cell phone he ever saw. It was his dad's, and it came in a briefcase. One day, his dad asked if he, a teenager at the time, wanted to run an errand with him. When the young man realized the phone would be joining them, he agreed.

Along the way his father stopped at a gas station, and when he disappeared to pay, the son pulled out the phone, called his best friend, and hung up just before his father got back in the car.

Whew. He felt pretty cool he had just called his friend from a car and even better that his dad would never know . . .

Except, of course, his father did find out.

A few weeks later when the bill arrived.

That thirty-second call cost three hundred dollars.

Innovation is amazing, but it can also be painful.

If ever you are struggling to find a story, turn to the nouns related to the message you wish to deliver. In fact, feel free to give this exercise a try right now.

Make a list of all the jobs you've ever had. Make a list of the all the homes you've ever lived in. Make a list of your teachers in school or coaches in sports. And with each noun you write down, take a moment. It's likely that a memory or two will come back to you. A memory that can be turned into a story.

Unlocking More Stories

Focusing on nouns is a great trick to help bring some stories to the forefront of your memory. Here are some additional prompts I use to help find the perfect story:

Think about firsts.

I'll never forget when I first met my husband. Or the first story I told. I'll never forget my first summer job or the first real storytelling keynote I gave. I'll never forget the first time a client called me absolutely giddy about the response they received from a story they told and the realization, as I hung up the phone, that perhaps this whole thing was bigger than I originally thought. I'll never forget my first real heartbreak or the first time I went to spin class. Behind each of these memories is an important story that could be told. In fact, I'm taking notes as I write. So many stories are coming back to me that I'd forgotten about.

If you're struggling to find your stories, shift your thoughts to the firsts in your life. They could be firsts that are related to the message you want to deliver in an obvious way (the first time you saw your product in action, the first day you were officially open for business, your first sales call) or a more distant way (the first time you tried a hobby you now love, the first time you met someone who is now important to you). The story you end up telling may not actually be about the first anything, but focusing on a first to begin with is a good way to unlock your memories and give you more story options.

Make a list of customer objections and questions.

This is often an awkward conversation. After hearing all the wonderful things a company does, I'll ask a client, "So why *don't* people choose you?" And while no one enjoys talking about this, if you know why your customer says no to what you have, you can tell stories that put their concerns at ease. If you know they think your product is too expensive, you know to look for stories that illustrate how your product saves them money in the long run. If you know they're resistant to change, you know to look for a story that illustrates the pain of not switching to your solution.

The same is true of the questions your potential customers ask most frequently. Think back to chapter 4 and the two systems in our brain— the one that goes with the flow and the other that gets called in to deal with the tough stuff. When we're asked a question, often our first instinct is to revert to answering with logic and, as a result, immediately get tangled up with System 2. If you know the most common questions people ask about your product or business ahead of time, though, you can find stories that answer them more effectively than a list of logical bullet points and help keep your customers in that far more desirable System 1 space.

Look for when you've seen your message in action.

My favorite thing about this prompt is it gives you the encouragement and freedom to look anywhere for your stories. If you want to deliver a message about perseverance, you can tell a story about a prototype that took many failed attempts before it finally worked. You could tell the story of how you wanted so badly to do the splits but couldn't until you finally figured it out after weeks and weeks of practicing in your bedroom and on the playground and at church. As long as you tie your story back to the message, almost anything is fair game.

Ask yourself lots of questions.

The number of stories you can find is limited only by the number of questions you ask yourself. Here is a list of questions I use to uncover stories that have otherwise been forgotten.

- When have you had to be resourceful in order to survive?
- What was the worst day in the history of your business?
- When have you made a customer cry? For good reasons? For bad?
- When have you stopped a customer from crying?
- What's the hardest thing you've ever done in business?
- Whose life is different because of your business?
- What is your proudest moment in your work or business?
- What one event or decision in your business history could your company not have survived without?
- When have you been surprised or mistaken about someone or something in your business?
- What was your first sale?
- What was your most meaningful sale?
- Do you remember a time when you lost a sale?
- Who is your most satisfied customer?
- Who is your most unsatisfied customer?
- What was your most embarrassing moment?

- When has someone said you couldn't accomplish something?
- What was the moment you knew the work you do is worth it?

Regardless of which of these prompts you choose, once you narrow down the list and start digging, you're going to find much more potential story material than you probably imagined was there.

The Great Lie

I was reading a book, and the author stated that, in order to have stories worth telling, you needed a life worth living, implying that the source of your storylessness is that your life isn't worth telling about. I will admit, while I'm not prone to physical expressions of anger, I threw that book across the room. Liar.

If this thought creeps in, ignore it.

It's a lie. A common lie. But a lie all the same.

Your life is full of stories. Which I know may sound bold, especially to someone who's sitting in front of a blank piece of paper, feeling like they don't have a story in the world and that nothing's ever happened to them that's worth telling about.

The truth is something I've said several times throughout this chapter: If you ever feel like you don't have stories, it's not because you don't; it's because our stories don't sound like stories to us. Our stories just sound like life. The finding exercises in this chapter will help distill specific moments and reveal them for what they really are: stories waiting to be found and told.

Finding the Story, Phase 2: Story Choosing

Yes, you have stories. If you work through the lists above you'll likely be overwhelmed with the possibilities. Or perhaps finding stories has never been your challenge. Maybe your challenge is that you've always known you have stories to tell, but you were just never sure where to start.

This brings us to the second part of finding stories. Now that you've collected some story options, you have to choose which story to craft and tell. That is what Suzanne and her company were facing. Not the problem of collecting but choosing.

For pet owners, few things are more difficult than having a dog or cat or other loved pet in need of care but not being able to afford it. That's an experience Suzanne Cannon knows all too well. When Suzanne's dog became seriously ill one weekend, her only option was an emergency veterinarian clinic. But just as it is for humans, when it comes to health-care for pets, *emergency* is another word for *expensive*. Before the weekend was out, Suzanne was facing a $4,000 bill that she had no idea how to pay.

At the time she was going through a bad divorce. Money was tight, and she couldn't get third-party financing because of her credit. The emergency clinic didn't accept payment plans.

What do you do if a loved one needs care you can't afford? It's a heartbreaking dilemma.

Suzanne's dog eventually recovered, but the agony of having a sick dog and no way to pay for care stuck with Suzanne. That was the beginning of VetBilling, which helps vets provide flexible payment options to pet owners.

Suzanne and her partner, Tony Ferraro, run VetBilling, and storytelling is a key part of their sales process. Unlike many companies that are still hoping features and benefits will get the job done, Suzanne was convinced they needed to connect on an emotional level. She has used her story from the beginning to illustrate the problem facing pet owners and vets and how VetBilling could help.

At first, things seemed to be working. They were signing up veterinarians to the VetBilling program without difficulty. But gradually a problem began to emerge. They had no revenue. Despite a number of vets on the roster, no money was coming in.

What Suzanne and Tony were running up against, they realized, was a deeper sales problem. While pet owners ultimately generated VetBilling's revenue through the use of the payment plans, the only way to get pet owners on plans in the first place was to have them referred by the vets. Even if a vet was signed up with VetBilling, nothing happened unless the vet used the program with their pet-owner clients. In essence, VetBilling needed the veterinarians to be fully engaged in order to succeed.

"When we first started," Tony said, "we would sign up ten clients in a month. But that doesn't mean that they would send us any payment plans. They'd say it was great and they understood it, but they wouldn't use us."

The VetBilling challenge was essentially the opposite of one that, say, a membership service like a gym might have. A gym just needs to sign people up—as many people as possible—for monthly membership plans, and then it doesn't matter if the client actually uses the gym. The gym still gets paid. Not so for VetBilling. The only way they make money is if their customers use the program.

The initial story had worked, but it hadn't solved the second part of the sales process—the part that means revenue for VetBilling and puts food on Suzanne's table and in her dog's bowl. How do you get the vets to use the service once they are signed up?

That was a problem for story to solve.

But not just any story. The right story.

Any Story Versus the Right Story

Suzanne's story, and the one she was telling the potential new veterinarians, was a classic founder story, and it was a great one. Her poignant personal experience had led to the creation of an entire business. It was compelling and authentic, and if you wanted reassurance that she was committed, her founder story did the job very well. But it wasn't growing VetBilling's revenue. Signing up was cost-free and risk-free. Vets could easily say yes, and they did. But getting the vets to use the service required a different story. A story that illustrated the value of using their service. A story that connected with the thing that kept vets up at night and showcased VetBilling as the solution to that problem.

Suzanne and Tony knew what that thing was: the heartbreaking act of turning a pet away because their owner couldn't pay. They knew veterinarians face all the challenging and tremendously stressful situations that many health-care professionals do. But they face an extra challenge that many doctors and nurses don't: almost no one has pet insurance. The industry is predominantly a cash business, and many pet owners simply cannot afford the cost of an unexpected visit.

Imagine you're a veterinarian. You almost certainly got into the business because of a love of animals. You empathize deeply with the bond between pet owners and their pets. But you're also running what is essentially a small hospital, complete with diagnostic equipment, surgical services, and inpatient care. It's expensive. You can't afford to make every pet a pro bono case.

What do you tell a pet owner who can't afford a life-saving procedure for their family dog? How do you walk the line between keeping your business solvent *and* helping every person and pet you want to?

After reflecting on the dilemma facing their clients, VetBilling shifted their story strategy to telling value stories, which changed everything. At the end of the day, it makes all the difference when you choose the right story for your situation rather than just any story.

―――

If your goal is to have more stories to tell at family events or at gatherings with your spouse's friends or on the sidelines of your kids' soccer games, then simply collecting stories would be enough. But when you want to use stories strategically, particularly in business, choosing the right story is equally as important, and a great place to start the choosing process is with the four essential stories we discussed in part 2 of this book. These stories are a straightforward way to narrow an infinite number of stories down to a few that serve a specific objective.

Here's a little cheat sheet:

- Choose a value story if you want more effective sales and marketing.
- Choose a founder story if you want to increase confidence and differentiate.
- Choose a purpose story if you want to align and engage your team.
- Choose a customer story if you want better sales, marketing, and credibility.

Over any reasonable period of time, most companies need all four stories. There's no enduring business that hasn't been through the process of being founded, growing sales, leading teams, and delivering service to customers. Additionally, the purpose of each story isn't exclusive. A great founder story, for example, can also serve to help sales. An awesome purpose story can drive sales too. The four stories overlap. But seeing them as distinct story types helps you get started choosing the right one.

So ask yourself which story you need the most right now. Which objective is most pressing? Once you narrow in on your objective, use the four stories as a guide to sift through the story options you discovered in the collecting process to find the one that best serves you.

This subtle but powerful shift to telling value stories was what VetBilling needed all along. Now, instead of focusing on the founder story, which still had its place of course, they began to build a collection of value stories from vets themselves. Stories that illustrated the true value of what was possible with VetBilling: the ability to fulfill every vet's ultimate desire to help as many pets as possible.

The results quickly followed.

"It tripled, quadrupled getting clients," Tony recalled. "Once we got the campaign rolling, it really expanded. Now, the veterinarians that we're signing up because of our stories, 95 percent of them are sending us business right away."

All About the Audience

What the VetBilling story teaches us is that making story work for your business is as much about choosing as it is telling. It's not enough to find a story. You need to pick the right one. The one that fits your needs, your business, and your audience.

That last one is key: your audience.

Remember, you're not telling a story for story's sake. And I certainly hope you're not telling a story just to hear your own voice. If you're telling a story in business, you're telling it to an audience for a reason. These are always my first two questions any time I sit down with a storytelling client:

1. Who are you telling this story to?
2. What do you want them to think, feel, know, or do?

The answers to these questions are an essential part of the story-choosing process. If the client is telling their story to new potential customers who might need some reassurance that this entrepreneur is the right person for the job, we choose stories that showcase the entrepreneur's competency and passion and have a dose of "you want what I have." If the audience is a boardroom of skeptical decision makers who care about and are doubtful of the effectiveness of the product, we'll choose a story of the product thriving under pressure and, if possible, include characters who were also skeptical but became believers after they said yes.

At its core, the art of choosing a story is all about knowing where the audience and your objective meet. Look through the moments you've collected, and choose a story that sits in that particular intersection and you're golden.

Finding Stories in the Moment

We have spent the majority of this chapter discussing ways to find stories that have happened in the past: moments in your history that could, with a little crafting, bring a bigger message to life and result in some big returns. But I would be remiss if I didn't mention my favorite way to find stories: watching them unfold before my eyes.

As I boarded a flight recently, I saw a little old lady, her sister, and a flight attendant in a battle over putting luggage in the overhead bin. Apparently, the elderly woman asked the flight attendant to put it up for her. The flight attendant said she wasn't allowed to per her contract. Maybe someone threw a punch? I'm not sure; I missed that part. But something big must have happened, because by the time I sat down, the flight attendant was threatening to remove the eighty-year-old and the sister from that flight.

Since I hadn't witnessed the beginning of the altercation, it was unclear who was at fault, but either way, the whole thing seemed a little extreme. Finally, as the flight attendant called the gate agent to make the removal, the sister was able to deescalate the situation by explaining that this was the first flight either of them had flown in many decades and they were unaware the policy had changed. The sister then told the story of the family reunion they were attending and how excited they were to be all together again.

The story saved the day. The flight attendant immediately softened and told a story about a recent family reunion she had attended. The sisters and the attendant discovered they shared Midwestern roots. They exchanged stories and contact information and hugged when we landed. I watched all of this unfold and thought that there was more than one story here. What I saw were stories about customer service, about jumping to conclusions, about misunderstandings, and how knowing someone's story leads to more connection, understanding, and compassion.

I made some notes about this interaction and thought that some-day I would tell this story. (Technically, I suppose that someday is here, although it's not for the purpose I originally intended.)

Now this story is a reminder that stories are happening around us every day. And now that you're well versed in the importance and value of stories, my hope is you'll be as addicted to finding new ones as I am.

To feed this addiction, all you need to do is put your cell phone down and look around. Any moment that makes you wonder could be a story. Or one that brings a smile to your face. Or one that makes you slightly angry. Or one that you watch unfold with heightened curiosity. Each of these is prime story material happening in the moment. The risk, of course, is that you'll forget it. The key to avoiding this fate is to quickly make note of what you saw or heard or witnessed.

This does not have to be a complicated process. In fact, my process for recording these moments is quite sloppy. Sometimes I jot a few thoughts down in my planner (yes, I still have one) or a small notebook (yes, I have one of those too) or in an app on my phone. Sometimes I email them to myself or post my thoughts as an Instagram story that only shows up for twenty-four hours and then is archived in my personal history for future reference. I scribble story scraps on napkins, the back of receipts, corners of pieces of paper that are laying around the house or in my bag.

My archive of stories is not neat. It's not pretty. And I vow to get better at it someday. In the meantime, I'll settle for at least having some kind of record of what I saw. And you should too.

However you choose to do it, take a moment to make note of the stories that are happening around you so you'll be more likely to remember the story scraps should the time come when you need to craft them into a story.

Once You Find What You're Looking For

I believe that was what I was looking at all those years ago at the storytelling festival in the moments before I welcomed my mentor to the stage. A list of scraps, collected over decades and ready to be told.

Of course, that's the difference. Donald Davis's list of scraps were more than just scraps. Each of them was ready to be told because he had taken the time to craft them.

That is our next step.

CHAPTER NINE

Crafting Your Story

How to Create Compelling Stories Even If You Don't Think You Can

Ideas come and go. Stories stay.
—NASSIM NICHOLAS TALEB, AUTHOR

When you do the work from the previous chapter, you'll end up with two things. The first is a collection of story ideas: the seeds of potential stories that you can use to captivate, influence, and transform. The second is a singular story idea: one that you chose from the collection as the best possible story idea for the job at hand.

Your next job is to craft that story in a way that makes it compelling for the person who will read it, hear it, or see it. As I reread that sentence, I realize this may sound intimidating if you've never considered yourself much of a writer. Perhaps you prefer formulas and equations. Or maybe you enjoyed journaling, but the last time you had to write anything other than an email or product description, you were still hopeful that *Lost* would have an adequate ending.

If this sounds like you, rest assured you can do this. I don't say this to flatter you. I say this because I've seen the most analytical, unemotional, self-proclaimed more-robot-than-human people craft unforgettable, irresistible stories. How? By using the system and components in this book. A formula you already know, a system you've seen in action with every story you've read here. Whether compelling storytelling is in your DNA or you eat data for breakfast, crafting great stories is a simple skill anyone can master.

Putting the Storytelling Framework and Components to Work

You remember our storytelling framework from chapter 3:

Normal ➜ Explosion ➜ New Normal

Three parts. Not nine. If you ask me, that's kinda nice. Nine seems like a lot. Three seems manageable. And as we'll see in this chapter, it totally is. Each one of these three parts plays an important role in crafting stories that will captivate, influence, and transform your audiences.

All you need are the story scraps you found in the previous chapter, mastery of the four components we've discussed throughout the whole book, and the story you've chosen to fit your objective. Once you have these elements in place, you'll be ready to start putting your story together. And although I'm usually the "let's start at the very beginning" type, when it comes to crafting a story, it's best to take what you found in chapter 8 and start in the middle.

Explosion: Start in the Middle

Though the explosion is the middle of our three-part framework, I find this is where our stories usually start. As you were looking for scraps of stories in the previous chapter, the memories, the moments that rose to the top were likely explosions, because when a story happens to us, more often than not, we don't recognize it until we're in the middle of it. We don't notice a story is happening until we get to the explosion. Which makes sense, because the first part of any given story is, by definition, normal. Hence the name. It's essentially not a story until the explosion happens, and as a result, we don't really notice the normal until we see it in contrast with the explosion and new normal.

This natural oblivion to the normal means it's a pretty tough place to start when crafting a story. Better to start with the explosion, the thing that happened, and then work backward.

For example, the explosion in the Workiva value story was when the aspiring athlete started using the Workiva product. The explosion for the financial advisor was when she was caught washing her money. The explosion for the dad trying to bestow wisdom on his daughter was when she pointed out he was wearing mismatched socks. As a sentence or a statement, none of these experiences, or explosions, are much of a story. They aren't going to draw you in and start the co-creative process; they aren't going to engage you in the emotions and the process of painting a collective mental picture.

But they are a place to start.

Once you identify that pivotal moment to build the story around, it's time to go back to the beginning.

Normal: Back to the Beginning

Crafting the normal is the most fun and most important piece of the story process. This is where you take a happening and make it matter. This is where you get to make your audience care. Additionally, this is where you get to flex your empathetic muscles, where you simultaneously say, "I know you" and "You know me." This is where the listener, reader, or hearer of your story settles in, lets down their guard, and if you do it right, blurs the lines between their world and yours long enough for you to bridge the gap.

And in case you're wondering, this is the part we humans love. Your audience will enjoy that subtle sense that, while everything appears to be going along as planned, something is about to happen. You see this play out a hundred times magnified when you watch a movie with someone who is extremely sensitive to the normal. Children are like this. My husband is like this too. It doesn't even have to be a thriller! All it needs is a steadily developing normal, and they can barely contain themselves. They have to ask questions. They have to make predictions. They are overwhelmed by the normal and know that something is about to explode, and they just can't handle it.

When it comes to business storytelling, it's much less dramatic than that but equally as effective.

The normal for the CEO of the Maricopa Medical Center was the developing scene at the community forum as the homeless man shuffled in, and we cared when they treated him differently than what we expected.

The normal for the boy in the McDonald's commercial was feeling like he had nothing in common with his father, so we cared when he found something they shared.

The normal for the water polo player was the entire story leading up to the moment he quit the team.

In each of these cases, the effect of the explosion was completely dependent on the crafting of the normal. And the same will be true for you and your stories. The good news is, you can use the story components as a checklist as you are building your normal.

Include details about the identifiable character, details that will paint the picture and sound familiar to the audience. Check!

Include the emotions, what they (or you if you're the character in the story) were feeling or hopeful for or thinking as the situation was unfolding. Check!

Include the particular moment in time and place that this was happening. A restaurant? A town hall? A regular Tuesday in mid-June? A stressful Friday during the holidays? Check!

And last, with your particular audience in mind, include details so it sounds familiar to them. Throughout the whole story they should be saying to themselves, *I've felt that. I understand that. That sounds about right. Yep. Yes. Yes. Yes.* Check!

Then, after all that yessing, when the explosion hits and the solution is found or the lesson is learned or the realization is had, the audience will say, "Oh—"

And much like in *When Harry Met Sally*, the next natural response is, "I'll have what she's having."

New Normal: Smooth Sailing

If you get the rest of the story right, the new normal writes itself. It's the recap of the lesson learned and what it means for the person hearing the story. As you craft the new normal, it's up to you how blatant you want to get about the message.

The water-polo-player-turned-executive didn't tell the audience not to give up or they'll regret it. But he implied it in the way he ended the new normal.

The Desert Star Construction founder finished his story by reminiscing about his first fort and saying that he couldn't wait to see what he and the new client might build together next.

The financial advisor assured her potential clients that she would treat their money with as much love as she had treated her own since she was a child.

The most important piece of crafting the new normal is to use it as an opportunity to come full circle. End the story back at the beginning, except with the benefit of the knowledge, wisdom, and understanding you didn't have in the normal.

There it is.

That's all you need to start crafting your stories. Like with anything, practice will make you better. Over time, either through external feed-back or your own, you'll get a sense for what works and what doesn't. And if you get the luxury of being able to tell a story more than once, perhaps in repeated pitches or in multiple interviews, use each telling as an opportunity to evaluate which pieces really hit the mark and which don't resonate as well and adjust as needed.

No Fine Print, No Gimmicks

The best part about using this proven method for crafting stories (besides the fact that it's as straightforward and simple as it sounds) is that it works. Fully. Completely. No tricks or gimmicks necessary.

Someone once approached me with a slight smirk after I spoke to a marketing audience.

"You changed the music, didn't you?" he said as he stood two inches from my face and stared at me.

"Uh . . . Ah . . . I'm . . ." I stuttered a bit, confused by the question and taken aback by the abruptness of it all.

The man didn't even introduce himself, he was so giddy about what he thought he'd figured out.

"In the after video. You changed the music to make it more emo-tional, didn't you?!" He smirked again.

Okay. It made sense now. In the presentation I had used an example of a brand who thought they were telling a story in one video and then showed the contrast in a second video when they actually did tell a story. The difference was profound, as you might expect. Apparently, the dif-ference was so profound this video marketing expert couldn't believe the distinction was made by the story alone. There must have been more to it. We must have changed the music as well to really drive home the contrast between the two stories.

"No," I answered with my own smirk. We had used the same track. The same footage. We only added some small clips, because the story version was slightly longer. All that had changed between the two videos was that we crafted a story and told it.

Well-crafted stories don't need gimmicks to work. That's the point!

Remember how I listened to the Juan and Sarah gum commercial on mute? Or how the Apple and Budweiser commercials didn't use words?

Any of the other stories in this book—and there have been a lot of them—have done the job not because we dressed them up or manipulated them in any way but rather because they were real, they included our necessary story components, and they followed this simple formula.

That is the beauty of storytelling. A story can just be itself.

Think how much better the world would be if we didn't have to approach each message with a smirk.

Story Anytime in Anytime

I'm often asked how long a story should be. The conversation can go a few different directions after this. Sometimes the person will mention the baby shoes story that may or may not have been written by Hemingway. I often mention the Mark Twain quote: "If I had more time, I would have written a shorter letter"—a nod to how much harder brevity is than length.

Perhaps the most aggravating answer I give is that a story should be as long as it needs to be.

For example, I recently stepped onto an elevator at the airport, and three people followed me: a young woman and two young men. They were going to the fourth floor. I was continuing on to the fifth.

The door closed, and the woman turned to her friends. "Do you know where my parents are right now?"

The guys shook their heads.

She said, "They're at a burial service for my grandfather's friend who died at Pearl Harbor. They just found the body, and they're going to pay their respects to good ol' Uncle Mike."

At that point the doors opened and the trio stepped off, leaving me alone in the elevator, my jaw on the floor. A Pearl Harbor victim just found now? I was so intrigued I almost jumped out after them, but the steel doors slammed shut, mocking both my curiosity and hesitation.

For decades, sales and marketing experts have been trying to solve the "elevator pitch" conundrum. How do you deliver enough information and create enough intrigue so that, in a short elevator journey with a prospect, they'd want to learn more?

Certainly, these travelers weren't trying to sell anything, but that's exactly the point. Their elevator pitch wasn't a pitch at all. It was a story.

Think about it. It had identifiable characters: the girl's parents and good ol' Uncle Mike. There was a moment in time: "right now." And even the specific detail of Pearl Harbor, which, like mentioning John F. Kennedy in the Eight & Bob story, is a shortcut to a whole world of familiarity for Americans.

I arrived home from the airport that evening and told my husband the story of the best elevator pitch ever—and admitted to almost losing a limb in the elevator shaft trying to chase them down to hear the rest. Together, we googled "Mike Pearl Harbor body found" and read about new DNA testing that meant families could finally lay their loved ones to rest. And, indeed, there had been a service that day—the one that young woman's parents were likely attending.

In truth, I don't think elevator pitches even matter that much. It's one of those sales techniques you hear about, but they never actually happen in the real world. What the story does reveal, though, is that stories don't have to be long to be effective. They just need to be as long as they need to be.

I know saying, "As long as it needs to be" is an annoying answer. But it's true. Like the story in the elevator, a story can be ten seconds or, if you were to attend the National Storytelling Festival in Jonesborough, Tennessee, and have the honor of hearing famed storyteller Jay

O'Callahan tell his story, "The Spirit of the Great Auk," you would be transfixed for ninety minutes. Yes, stories can be as long or as short as you need them to be as long as they follow the framework and include the components.

I find the best approach is to start with the whole story. Write it out, tell it all, hold nothing back. From there, cut it back to fit the space you have. Here are a few examples of what that might look like.

The Ten-Second Story

The ten-second story for Unbounce, for example, might be:

> A marketing manager struggled to do his job with little budget, technical savvy, and control. He was frustrated, felt undervalued, and if he was totally honest, he was a little pissed. Then he started using Unbounce Convertables. Now he can do everything he wanted to, with the skills he has, well within budget, and he doesn't hate his job anymore. If he's totally honest, he loves it again.

Let's take inventory on that one:

- **Normal:** Struggling to do his job.
- **Explosion:** Using Unbounce Convertables.
- **New Normal:** Can do his job and enjoy it. Also note the tie-in with the normal by replicating the phrase "If he's totally honest," but with the opposite result.
- **Identifiable Character:** A specific marketing manager.
- **Emotion:** Frustration, feeling undervalued, pissed.
- **Moment:** Started using Convertables.
- **Specific Details:** It doesn't use a specific physical detail to drive the sense of familiarity, but by including the word *pissed*, it taps into the vernacular of that persona, likely a millennial who would express their feelings that way.

The ten-second story for VetBilling might be:

Lisa dreamed of being a veterinarian her whole life. She had no idea how heartbreaking it would be to not be able to help financially strapped owners whose beloved pets desperately needed services they couldn't afford. Then Lisa found VetBilling. Now she doesn't have to worry about saying no to pets in need and is free to do the work she was born to do.

Here's another inventory check:

- **Normal:** Dreams of being a vet. Not being able to help pets whose owners couldn't pay.
- **Explosion:** Finding VetBilling.
- **New Normal:** Now she can serve all pets. Also note the tie-in with the normal when we mention her lifelong dream and then her ability to do the work she was born to do.
- **Identifiable Character:** Lisa the vet.
- **Emotion:** Heartbreak.
- **Moment:** This story doesn't include a specific moment (which isn't ideal, but with a super short story, often one of the components gets cut).
- **Specific Details:** Like the Unbounce story, this one doesn't include a specific physical detail. But the heartbreak is a familiar and specific emotion veterinarians experience.

To go from the full story to ten seconds is pretty extreme. And the chances you'll actually talk to someone in an elevator are slim. Typically, stories in business range from three to seven minutes in length, and it's your job to spend those minutes wisely. Those minutes are best spent building out the normal with the components, drawing your audience into the co-creative process, helping them create a compelling picture in their minds, connecting them with the emotions and what's at stake, and getting them to say, "I understand that" and "I can relate to that."

If you do that, time won't matter. It will stand still.

Avoiding Common Crafting Pitfalls

Even with a framework and components as simple as what you've learned here, there are a few common missteps and temptations to avoid. Knowing them up front will help you in the process.

Not Crafting the Story to Specifically Support Your Goals

In 2015, I did a workshop for the United Way in Indianapolis. The audience that day was made up almost entirely of fund-raisers, which was particularly fun and challenging because the room was filled with what amounts to professional storytellers. While my job is often to help people who are just beginning to use stories, this was an opportunity to help professional storytellers raise their game.

Most days, the job of a fund-raiser is really one of sales. To raise funds for United Way programs, they might have a one-on-one meeting with a decision maker or donor one day and speak to an entire room of corporate employees the next. But in each case, it's their stories that help them do their work.

We spent a day working on those stories, and I came back the following June to check in and take things a step further. By that point, they'd been applying the previous workshop strategies for almost a full year, and it was time for some advanced tactics.

The day's plan was simple. Four people would share the stories they'd been using, and we'd workshop them together, enhancing them, refining them, and sharing what was working and what wasn't.

Sharon (not her real name) told a beautiful story about a little boy she'd worked with when she'd first been a volunteer reader with the United Way. When she met the boy, he was debilitatingly shy and withdrawn, but over the course of their time together, he emerged from his shell and began to thrive.

It was a killer story that perfectly illustrated the possibility for change that United Way could offer, and Sharon had the room captivated. After much ado, I got ready to move to the next story. Sharon had clearly nailed it.

But after the accolades and before I welcomed the next teller, Sharon raised her hand. "Here's the problem I'm having," she said. "I'm not getting donations."

"Do you tell it just like that?" I asked.

"Yes. And I know people love the story. Some people get close to tears."

I was confused. What was the problem?

"The problem," Sharon explained, "is that they all want to become volunteers."

At first blush that sounds impressive. Getting volunteer help is notoriously challenging. And United Way always needs volunteers. But that wasn't Sharon's goal. The programs need money, and Sharon's job was to raise it. Her story, as beautiful and touching as it was, simply wasn't doing the job she needed it to. It was doing *a* job, but the wrong one.

Just as we learned in the previous chapter, there is a difference between finding *a* story and finding the *right* story. I was confident Sharon had found the right story; the story about the boy and the difference United Way had made in his life was perfectly suited for the task at hand. What we were dealing with was a crafting issue. As we rewound her story and worked through it, the problem jumped out right away. The story itself was compelling, but the message in her story—what people took away—was that it's very rewarding to volunteer.

Her normal trended strongly toward what it felt like for her to volunteer. She was the identifiable character. It was her emotions. The moment and explosion were centered around her realization about the value of volunteering. A simple shift to make the boy the character, to focus on his emotions and the transformation that was made possible by the money donated by people like those Sharon presents to, changed the story completely. And yet not at all. The story was still essentially the same; it was the crafting that shifted.

Sharon's problem is an important one and illustrates the nuances that come with crafting the story right. Fortunately, rarely do you have to scrap an entire story. If you ever feel confident you have found the right story, but it's not hitting the mark, take a look at how you've crafted it. Do you have the right character? Is your explosion aligned with your objective? With just a few small tweaks, Sharon was back in business, and you can be too.

Cutting the Small Stuff

"It's missing something."

That's all my friend said in his email. We'd been working together to find the perfect opening story for his upcoming presentation about financial independence, and we had found one: the story of opening his first bank account as a kid with his grandmother.

It had all the makings of a great story. He (as a child) was the identifiable character (people love that, by the way, especially when you're in a leadership position). There was a powerful lure into the co-creative process with details such as sitting across from the banker, the checkbook, even the candies on the desk. It was perfect.

My friend sent the draft to his team of editors for a final review, and that's where it all fell apart. The version they sent back still had the story, but it fell flat. So flat the audience would likely wonder why he told it in the first place.

"It's missing something," he said. He was right. What was missing? All the details. The meticulous nuances that made the story an actual story. The editors had gone through and scrubbed the document clean of the finer points, the components our research shows are critical to a great story. A once vibrant tale was now a generic shell of events: Boy wants to buy things, boy opens bank account, boy understands money. Hollow and forgettable.

Whether you have a team of editors or you're the one with the proverbial red pen, beware the temptation to delete what matters most. After everything you've learned here, I know there's likely that voice in the back of your head that is obsessed with brevity: 140 characters (now 280, by the way) and 15-second clips. And this obsession means some of the most engaging parts of your stories are still at risk.

If ever you feel your story might be missing something, take a look on the cutting room floor to make sure you didn't get rid of the most important parts. As for the banking story, we reinserted the missing details and breathed life back into it. Yes, it took a few more words, but they were the ones that mattered most.

The Best for Last

There is a lot to love about our method for crafting stories. It's simple. It's straightforward. It works. But my favorite thing, the thing that makes writing this how-to chapter worth it (I'll be honest, I'm not a huge fan of writing how-to chapters) is that using this method for crafting stories means any moment can become a story. Any happening or realization from your past. Any incident that happens on a Tuesday and makes you say, "Huh?"

Anytime you're in the middle of a mess, you're actually a story in the making. No matter how small the moment, if you craft it in the way I've outlined and match it to your message, you've got a possible story on your hands.

I was recently visiting my sister-in-law at her office in a San Francisco high-rise. She walked me past each cubicle, and as she did, she introduced me as "that storyteller I told you about." Everyone smiled with recognition, and I felt a deep sense of gratitude for having my sister-in-law's support. We approached one woman, and my sister-in-law said, "This is my brother's wife. She's the one whose book of stories I gave you a while back," referring to a collection of stories I'd written in 2012. The woman looked at me, and her face lit up.

"That story! That story about when you were in middle school and went outside! I love that story. I think of it often. It really impacted me."

I was taken aback for several reasons. First, I certainly wasn't expecting this kind of welcome on a tour of my sister-in-law's office. But more importantly, I couldn't believe that story had that kind of impact. It was such a small one. A tiny moment from when I was in sixth grade.

———

Sixth grade was a hard year for me. It was the first year of middle school. I was slightly eccentric for my age in an environment where even a fraction of differentness was grounds for ridicule. Looking back, I'm not sure I had a single friend. And then, as if by miracle, I was cast in a neighboring school district's high school play, *The Sound of Music*.

I was Marta von Trapp, the second youngest child. As far as I was concerned, that role saved my life.

While junior high kids seemed to despise me, the high school kids playing nuns, Nazis, and a traveling-singing troop of siblings seemed to adore me. They talked to me. They laughed with me. They encouraged me. They wanted to be my friend. During the course of those few months I felt like myself again. I could be silly and creative and no one seemed to care.

In a time when I almost lost myself, somewhere in the hills alive with music I was safe. The show ran for two weekends, and on the last night I dreamed the curtains would malfunction, making them impossible to close so the show would go on. Forever. And I could be Marta for the rest of my life, or at least the rest of sixth grade.

That last night, I was invited to the cast party at one of the nun's houses. Despite the fact I was only eleven, my mother and father allowed me to go to a party with the high school kids who made me so happy. It was a chilly fall night, and the party host's father took us all on a hayride through the fields and forest behind their rural home. Afterward, we came in, sat in the basement, drank cider and hot chocolate with marshmallows, and ate Cool Ranch Doritos and pizza.

I was glowing with joy when the girl who played Louisa von Trapp (my singing sibling) took me by the hand and brought me into the yard in front of the house. Louisa had been one of my favorites in the play; she was tall and thin with long golden blond hair and bright blue eyes. Her face was innocent, like a Cabbage Patch doll who had shed her baby fat and now could sing and dance and drive a car. We sat in the grass for a bit, and then Louisa asked me if I wanted to try something cool. I said yes. While many a story that starts this way ends with the first time someone smoked or drank or something like that, this isn't that kind of story.

Louisa told me to get on my hands and knees. I did. I could see my breath as it froze in the space between my lips and the ground. She told me to close my eyes. I did. She told me to feel the earth in my hands below me. I could. It was cold and hard and wet and prickly. It was getting ready for winter, for the first snow that would come only a few days later, erasing any evidence we had been there.

Then Louisa told me to imagine, instead of just kneeling there on the grass, a bystander on the earth, that I was *holding* it. That as I felt the cold ground beneath me, it was actually in the palm of my hand. She told me to recognize that, at this moment, on this piece of earth, I was holding the world up with my own two hands. I opened my eyes with my hands firmly entangled in the grass, holding on for dear life. The world had never looked so new.

Louisa spoke softly then, as if to herself, as if she knew the pain of being eleven, being in sixth grade, of not wanting to wear a training bra, and of the cruelty of other children. As if she knew that the world can be tough beyond sixth grade. On all fours herself, she whispered that when the world was getting the best of you, all you had to do was take a moment to hold it in the palm of your hands. That's how you know you still have a place. That even if it's just this one piece of land where your hands are planted, there is a place for you and the possibilities for you are infinite.

As I stood in front of the woman's cubicle in San Francisco, I remembered that story, that moment, that feeling. I saw it reflected in my sister-in-law's coworker's eyes, and I remembered that night from many years earlier. I remembered walking back to the house in my last few minutes as Marta, hand in hand with Louisa, and the way both our eyes glistened in the dampness of the nighttime air. And I remembered how that collection of five random minutes from sixth grade could have such an impact.

―――

These instances happen to us daily. Small lessons, little events, collections of minutes where we learn something new or understand things in a different way. Minutes we might otherwise forget.

Except now you're a storyteller.

Now you know that stories are what matter most.

Now you know the more stories you can tell, the more effective you'll be.

And you might have been a little concerned if you don't have enough stories. What if you only have one or two, and you want more? How do you get them?

Let my story from sixth grade be all the assurance you need. Because that moment could have been lost in the shuffle of life; it was only the crafting of the story around that explosion that made it matter to the woman in my sister-in-law's office.

That's the power of crafting. When you're equipped with the framework and proven components, no matter the length, no matter the seeming smallness of the moment. If crafted well, any story is possible.

And it's my hope you'll tell them.

Which is what we'll cover next.

CHAPTER TEN

Telling Your Story

Where, When, and How
to Tell Your Stories

Storytelling is as old as the campfire, and as young as a tweet.

What moves people is someone who is credible.

—RICHARD BRANSON, FOUNDER OF THE VIRGIN GROUP

If a tree falls in a forest and no one is around to hear it, does it make a sound?

It's an age-old question, and when it comes to your stories, a relevant one.

If you find your story and put the effort into crafting it, but you never tell it, does it even matter? While the forest-tree conundrum is up for debate, the answer to the storytelling question is pretty straightforward.

No.

When it comes to storytelling, simply knowing all the things you've learned thus far does you no good. Knowledge is not power; it's just wasted brain space if you never actually tell your story.

The good news is that your opportunities for storytelling are endless and ever-growing. Case in point: A recent *Wall Street Journal* article announced that some companies are now printing inserts and paying to have them included in packages from retailers such as Saks Fifth Avenue and Zulily.[1] If you're going to spend that much money on an ad, you might as well tell a story and make it worth it.

And much like Windex, duct tape, or in my opinion, a nice glass of champagne, a well-told story can solve a whole variety of challenges in business and beyond. Essentially, when in doubt, tell a story. This has basically been my mantra for the past two decades.

For example, I used to be a spin instructor, which, I should start by saying, is a lot more intense than you might expect. There is so much going on in that single hour of teaching: you have to remember the movements, change the lighting, call out instructions, adjust the music volume, keep the riders motivated when all they really want to do is die, and, oh yeah, be a cardio machine.

And that's just during the class. Perhaps the most stressful part of teaching a spin class is putting together the playlist ahead of time. I don't know if you've ever been to a workout class where the music was insufferable, but it is a unique form of cruel and unusual punishment that should be reserved for the likes of evil dictators.

I'll never forget the terror of putting my first few playlists together. Would the riders like it? What if they hated Britney Spears and Daft Punk? Every week when I got on the instructor bike, I had a pit in my stomach about this. To ease it, out of instinct, I started telling stories. Before each set, while the riders were hydrating, I would tell a story about the song that was about to play next. They were short, funny, and added context to every ride. So, yeah, maybe they hated Kylie Minogue, but they loved the story I told about picking Michael up from the airport before we were dating and blasting "Can't Get You Out of My Head" from my car in an effort to be subtle.

Slowly but surely, what started out as just a few riders at 9:30 a.m. on Sunday mornings and 6:45 p.m. on Wednesday nights turned into sold-out classes and people being turned away at the door. And when I taught my final class two years later, my riders said they'd miss the workout, yes, but the thing they'd miss most was my stories.

When in doubt, tell a story. Tell them in emails and email campaigns. Leave a story in a voice mail. Tell a story in your autoresponder. Tell them in meetings. Tell stories in webinars. Tell them online. A 2014 study conducted jointly by social ad tech firm Adaptly and Facebook and Refinery29, a fashion and style website, concluded that telling a brand story—bringing customers through a sequential series of messages—was more effective than simply using traditional calls to action. Not just more effective, but *way more* effective, with the storied approach leading to a ninefold increase in view through and subscription rates.[2]

So tell, tell, tell. Be the one who people look forward to hearing from, even if they can't quite put their finger on why. You know why. Because people love stories. They want stories. So go ahead. Give them what they want. Tell your stories.

Here are a few insights on how, where, and when to do it.

Tell Stories in Presentations

One of the most obvious places to tell your stories is in presentations. Whether it's a five-minute update at a weekly team meeting or an eight-hour pitch to close a multimillion-dollar sale, stories will make your presentation and subsequent results better. Here are a few tips.

Start with a Story

It was a Thursday afternoon, and I was catching up with friends during a rare happy hour. Shelly is an expert in her field and had just started speaking at conferences in her industry. That visibility has meant excellent growth for her business, but for someone who never considered herself a public speaker, each presentation was intimidating. She asked if I had any advice. You won't be surprised to hear I told her to tell a story, but my reasons and strategies were far more specific than you might expect. Specifically, I insisted she start with a story.

The moment she stepped on stage and greeted the room, I told her to immediately launch into her story. Why? Several reasons. One, it's an easy way to ease the natural tension that sometimes exists between audience and speaker. Sometimes the nature of the event—a pitch or sales presentation—puts an automatic divide between the two. At other times the nature of the audience makes the environment a little hostile. Perhaps the audience is comprised of experts in the field who are skeptical about listening to other so-called experts. In either case, starting with a story helps to break down these barriers and makes you a person just like them instead of the expert in front of the room they are forced to listen to.

To that end, I encouraged Shelly to tell a story that centered on a client versus herself and her expertise, whose situation was likely one the audience had experienced themselves. Or tell a story of one of her kids. As we've learned in previous chapters, as long as the major lesson learned with her children was relevant to the overall message of her presentation, it could work to both illustrate a point and equalize or neutralize any audience tension.

Starting with a story also helps to calm your nerves and for good reason. The act of public speaking, being on display and vulnerable to people's judgment and criticism, often triggers the ancient self-preservation fight-or-flight response. Starting with a story answers the only question a speaker's lizard brain cares about in that moment: Do they like me?

If you start your presentation with a story—the thing other people love hearing—you will see the audience naturally engage, nod their heads, uncross their arms, perhaps even chuckle. Not only is this a positive experience for the people listening to you, the visual cues of acceptance will signal your ancient self that, yes, people like you. With that question answered, the rest of the presentation gets a whole lot easier.

Shelly thanked me for the advice that night and vowed to put it into practice. Four days after our conversation, she sent me a text. Based on the excessive number of emojis and extreme capitalization, I could tell she was still on a speaker's high. She wrote, "I started with a story about my daughter and it was FANTASTIC!" After the lecture she was swarmed by people who said it was the best presentation they'd ever heard. A presentation destined for success from the moment it began.

When a Picture Is Not Worth a Thousand Words

There was a time early in my speaking career when I refused to have a PowerPoint or slide deck. I claimed it was because I was a storyteller and my edge was that I could make a compelling presentation without technical assistance. The real reason was I was terrified of PowerPoint and technical difficulties. But after a few presentations, I had the distinct impression that, although the audience enjoyed my stories, they were having a hard time following the accompanying points. Reluctantly, I started using PowerPoint. Now I have slides for almost every presentation I give, and I am a firm believer that, done right, a slide deck is an extremely effective tool for keeping both you and the audience on track.

Please note the words "done right" in the previous sentence. They are important. Because done wrong means certain death to many of your presentation dreams. Here are a few key pieces of advice to make sure your deck and your stories work together in perfect presentation harmony.

First, make sure you leave dedicated space in your deck for the stories. Think of it as a slide that signals "Story Goes Here." Perhaps you're going to tell a story about the day you founded your company; include a slide that is simply your logo. The audience sees a logo and you see the signal to tell the story. Include these story slides throughout the deck as constant reminders to shift from the bullet points and data and information to the stories that make that information matter.

Second, while a story slide is a great reminder to switch to a story, choose the image wisely. Where a digital presentation becomes a problem for storytelling is when you rely on the images on the slides to tell your stories instead of your telling them for yourself. Remember, an audience's favorite thing about hearing a story actually occurs subconsciously. While you tell a story, the imagination of each listener creates the imagery to go along with it. They pull from meaningful material and experiences in their own lives to create this imagery so that, in the end, what the audience is left with is a meld of your words and their memories.

This is how your message sticks.

Which is why I warn you to choose your images wisely. The temptation is often to, while you tell a story, flash photos from the story on the screen. Telling a story about your kids? Here's a picture. Telling a story about you waterskiing? Here's a picture. And while that seems like the way to go, it creates a cognitive bypass and, in doing so, violates the power of the co-creative process. Give them the image and they won't create it for themselves. And now you've lost your cognitive edge.

I heard a speaker talk about his dream home, and he did an exquisite job of describing it. From how big it was to the picturesque windows to the way the streets looked as you gazed out the picturesque windows. He was describing his dream house, but I was imagining *my* dream house. And then he posted a picture of his dream house on the screen. He said, "See, there it is. There's my dream house."

I looked at the picture and thought, *Oh. That's not what I pictured. But okay.* And in that moment, all the work he'd put into engaging me in the co-creative process was wasted.

To avoid this mistake, when you tell a story in a presentation, use your words instead of relying on the images in your deck. Instead of putting up a picture of your kids, simply describe them, and the audience will, no matter how different your kids are, imagine their own. And when you choose an image for your story slide, choose a nondescript one that still gives room for the audience to create their own.

The good news is that storytelling and slide decks play well together. The combination satisfies both visual and aural learners, as long as you give yourself the cue to tell the story and then actually tell it, with your words, instead of relying on pictures to do it for you. No one enjoys watching someone flick through photos of their family vacation. They won't enjoy it in your presentation either.

Practice Breaks Perfect

In 2008, I was chosen for a once-in-a-lifetime opportunity to tell on the biggest traditional storytelling stage there is: the annual National Storytelling Festival in Jonesborough, Tennessee.

For traditional storytellers, it's the Super Bowl of story. If I nailed it, I was guaranteed an endless supply of stages on which to tell my stories and eternal storytelling glory. Mess it up, and I'd be forgotten forever. There were no second chances. I had eight make-or-break minutes to launch my storytelling performance career.

I immediately started practicing. I practiced daily. Every word. I woke up thinking about my story. I told it to my rearview mirror as I drove. I said it in the shower. I fell asleep each night with my own voice in my head telling my story over and over.

When the day arrived, the practice paid off: I delivered my story flawlessly. I didn't forget a single word. No "ums" or "uhs." No stutters or stammers. I was thanked and escorted off the stage.

And then I went home, knowing I'd blown it.

My big storytelling opportunity in Tennessee was a perfect example of how we can sabotage our natural storytelling ability. I lost that day, not because I didn't practice enough or because I made too many mistakes. I lost because I was too practiced.

I had fallen for the myth of the perfect speech. That when it comes to telling stories, practice makes perfect. Instead, right now, I want you, like Goldilocks and the three bears, to strike that balance between being well prepared (because winging it is almost always disastrous) and being over-rehearsed so that your stories are just right. How do you get there, to that just-right spot?

The key is to focus on your message, not the words. Think more about the message you're making with your story and less about the exact words you use to do it. Yes, you should practice. You must practice. But practice until you're prepared, not perfect. Leave room for spontaneity. For audience reaction. Let go of perfect and it will let go of you.

While, as of this writing, I have not yet been invited back to tell at the National Storytelling Festival, I'm hopeful that day will come.

Tell Stories to Get Ahead

Regardless of the position you're in and the position you're going for, whether you're looking to rise through the ranks or secure the position in the first place, you will likely encounter varying forms of the interview process. You'll face the daunting task of having to communicate the very essence of the person you are, the value you bring to an audience that is required to be skeptical. How do you answer these questions? You tell stories.

Several years ago, I heard from a young man who was familiar with and had been casually following my work in storytelling. Matt was a fighter pilot, and when he reached out, he was making the transition from flying for the military to flying for a commercial airline. He was in the middle of the interview process.

I wasn't aware at the time, but the process was pretty high stakes. Pilot positions are highly coveted and extremely competitive. Usually, there's just one position and a long line of qualified applicants. To rise to the top, Matt was acutely aware he had to stand out in a way the other Tom Cruise lookalikes didn't.

As you might expect, there were various elements to the hiring process, and one of them was a grueling interview. He decided to make story his strategy.

"Tell us a little bit about yourself." Instead of rambling, Matt was ready with a story that illustrated his skills, passion, and character.

"Tell us of a time you were in a stressful situation and how you responded." Matt had a story ready.

"What do you feel are the most important leadership skills?" Matt had a story.

For every single question, he was ready with another story to make himself memorable, to connect with this very critical crowd, and to rise above the rest of the competition.

The interview was in the morning. When it was complete, Matt took a test and then settled in for a painful waiting game that lasted until 3:30 p.m. Before the day was over, Matt was offered a position with the first-choice airline of every would-be pilot. He sent me a message that evening that he had put some of my storytelling strategies to work and secured his dream job.

That was an important reminder for me that I now pass on to you: Never underestimate the power your story has over the competition. When the stakes are highest, come prepared to tell stories and watch the results follow.

Tell the Story That Feels Right to You

A few years ago, I worked with a young company named Soul Carrier that produced unique handbags for women. At the time, Soul Carrier was using a video to tell their story, and while it was a well-produced piece, it committed a classic storytelling mistake: it wasn't really a story.

I worked with Soul Carrier to rework the video—to tell the story of a young woman who lost her parents and, for a time, her way. It's a powerful founder story that touches on loss, finding your path, and redemption. It's moving, raw, and authentic. And, of course, it's a story.

It's an extreme story, and I often use the Soul Carrier example in my keynotes as a way to illustrate, without a doubt, the impact telling a story can truly make. And while that is the main lesson, a secondary one is also at play.

When it comes to telling stories, only tell the stories you are comfortable telling.

I was confronted with this lesson at a recent event when a woman approached me in the lunch buffet line after my keynote. She was the head of a prominent, extremely successful nationwide charter school system. As part of her role, she frequently spoke to audiences about her school and their methods, values, and impact. She approached me with some concern, namely that the Soul Carrier story seemed too personal and a bit exploitative.

She explained she had hundreds of stories of students who came from broken homes and challenging environments who had thrived. But she didn't want to tell those stories. She felt they were confidential, and she also felt that using them would be wrong.

I sensed in her tone that she felt conflicted about this. People had probably told her she should tell these stories; after all, those are the kinds of stories people really want to hear. Entrepreneurs also struggle with this. Perhaps they faced extreme adversity in their lives and were able to rise above it. But regardless of how good the story is, sometimes it doesn't match the message, or in other cases, you just don't want the world to know that story.

In that case, I tell people don't tell it.

"Don't tell those stories" is exactly what I told the educator in the buffet line as I put a second chicken taco on my plate.

She looked at me, a little surprised.

"Only tell the stories that feel right and ready to be told."

Of course, this didn't let her off the hook of telling stories at all. Instead, I told her to tell stories about the teachers who are committed to these students. The teacher stories were a better fit for her message anyway. Her audience is primarily educators, and her message is always about innovative models and tools in teaching that her schools use to get great results.

There is a certain pressure that comes with knowing you should be telling stories. And there is a common misconception that if you have dramatic or painful stories at your disposal, you must tell them. But as we've learned in the previous two chapters, using the right story is as important as using any story. Additionally, and perhaps more importantly, your stories are your own. Only you can choose which ones to tell. My hope is that you will choose one that feels right to you. You'll take a chance, and you'll tell it.

Get Out of Your Own Way

Here is one final, surprising truth about storytelling. If you look back at the times when things went well, it was often when you were telling a story. When you were happiest. When you felt the best. When you were rocking it out, closing the sale, winning the girl/boy, getting the gig, you were likely telling a story.

When you have a great story to tell, the telling simply becomes an afterthought. When you have a real story to tell, the telling is as natural as waking up. All the fears we have around storytelling are formed because we're not taught, told, or even allowed to use our natural story ability and style. We aren't encouraged to tell stories. Instead, we're encouraged to write reports, dig up facts, show our work, get the format right, and speak without "um"-ing.

Get the story right and the telling will come. How many times have you sat with a friend over a glass of wine and poured out a story? A heartwarming one about your child? A heartbreaking one about your relationship? There's no doubt you told that story with the eloquence of a master. Because that's what you are! Storytelling is a natural ability for humans. All you need is to get out of your own way. Almost all the problems in storytelling aren't so much story problems as they are problems with the teller getting in the way of the story. Find a real story that resonates with you, and it will almost tell itself.

Conclusion

Happily Ever After Is
Just the Beginning

Great stories happen to those who can tell them.
—IRA GLASS

When my son was about two and a half years old, he didn't appear to care much about trucks, but every night before bed he demanded that we read *Goodnight, Goodnight Construction Site*, a rhyming children's book that takes no fewer than thirty minutes to read.

For months, hundreds of nights in a row, my sweet son would sit on my lap in his little pajamas as I tried to find new ways to abbreviate the story without his noticing.

But kids always notice.

Finally, one night I simply couldn't take it anymore. When he crawled into my lap holding *Goodnight, Goodnight Construction Site*, I pleaded with him.

"Please, *please* can we read a different book?"

"I want *Construction Site*," he replied.

Evil little dictator, I thought. "What about the ducklings book or *Goodnight Moon*?"

"*Construction Site.*"

There was clearly no negotiating.

Just before I was about to throw my own version of a two-and-a-half-year-old tantrum, I had an idea.

"What if I told you a story?"

I'd never tried before, but I was a professional, after all.

"*Construction Site.*"

"What if I told you a story about when Mama was a little girl . . ."

The bossy king hesitated. I seized the opportunity.

"Every night when Mama was a little girl and it was the summertime, she would lay in her bed until the sun went to sleep and the sky was dark. Then she would sneak out of her bed, tiptoe to the front door, and sneak outside. Mama lived way out in the country where there were trees everywhere and short grass and tall grass, and the sky was so big and dark blue. And when she looked at the sky, she could see millions and billions of tiny twinkling stars. But Mama's favorite thing about the summer nights was walking out into the warm, wet air and onto the cool, wet grass, and all around her, in the darkness, danced hundreds of tiny blinking green lights . . . Fireflies!"

I told my son how I played with the fireflies. How I caught them and how they crawled on my hands and climbed through my hair. And then I would tell the fireflies goodnight and see you tomorrow and tiptoe back to my room and fall asleep.

The story didn't have a complicated plot or *any* plot for that matter. It wasn't long, and it didn't require anything of my imagination. I simply told him one of my favorite memories of being a child.

The story worked. My son sat still, silently. He barely breathed. Looking back, he strongly resembled the way his father looked in that Slovenian shop a few years later. Totally captivated for the first time in his two and a half years. When the story was done, he asked me to tell it again. And again.

"Tell me about the fireflies, Mama."

We haven't talked about construction sites since.

Now the only thing that satisfies this child is a story. My stories. His father's stories. His grandparents' stories. If I didn't know better, I would blame myself for a creating a monster—a monster with an insatiable appetite. But go ahead, try to feed him Goldfish or applesauce. He'd only throw it back at you. He wants stories.

Of course, I know it's not my fault, and to be clear, he's not a monster. Which, I suppose, is the point. My son wants to hear stories because he's human. And though he's no longer two years old (and likes to frequently point out that he's almost taller than me), he still wants stories. He asks for stories about when my husband got hurt as a kid. He asks for stories about my favorite thing to do while I was growing up.

One time, when he had his first splinter but refused to let me pull it out, he was desperate to make sense of what was going to happen next. So he asked me with a shaky voice on our drive to the school drop-off, "Mama, do you have a story about when you had a splinter?" Unfortunately, I didn't have a story, or at least not one I could remember. Disappointed, he walked into the classroom, splinter still in his hand. I called Michael.

"Our boy asked for a story about a splinter, and I didn't have one! Ultimate parenting fail."

"Oh!" Michael responded, "I have one of those." Michael grew up sailing. "I used to always get splinters in my feet when I would run up and down the docks in bare feet! I'll tell him that story when I get home."

Besides the fact that this exchange confirmed that we truly are meant to be together, even though Michael's not much of a shopper, it was also an important reminder that our lives are all story. A real-life narrative that we're constructing day by day, piece by piece in an effort to make sense of the world, find our place in it, and perhaps find a little happiness along the way.

My son asks for stories as a way to make sense of things that have happened or might happen to him. It isn't just something we do or need. Stories are what we are.

Remember that when it comes to storytelling in business, you're not reinventing the wheel; you're dipping into the current of story that runs through our heads and our lives all the time. And that's a current worth dipping into—in business and beyond.

In fact, a 2016 study by some researchers at the University of North Carolina at Chapel Hill and SUNY Buffalo found that people who are good at storytelling are also more attractive. Results from this study specifically concluded that women find men who are good storytellers to be more attractive and better long-term partners. The researchers surmised this was because "storytelling ability reflects a man's ability to gain resources. Good storytellers may be more likely to influence others or to gain positions of authority in society."[1]

Whether at home with your family, trying to find a mate, or getting ahead in your career, story is the way to do it.

After all, storytellers get hired. They win the contract.

Storytellers make the sale. Get the boy. Get the girl.

Storytellers survive the onslaught. They hold court. Capture attention. Win accolades. Move to tears.

Storytellers close the gap.

Become one and you will close the distance between what you have and what you want. You shrink the space between where you are and where you want to be in business and in life.

Once Upon a Time . . .

As our time together comes to a close and you prepare to go off and build your bridges, allow me to leave you with the one phrase many stories have started with since the beginning of time. These are some of the best stories, you might argue. But the stories that begin with "Once upon a time" are often fairy tales. They aren't true, and they certainly aren't business.

But once upon a time, something did happen. It happened to you. Or maybe your partner. It happened to your employees. Your vendors. And it happened to your customers.

Once upon a time, a failed marketing effort left you cashless, and then . . .

Once upon a time, you ran completely out of money, and then . . .

Once upon a time, a critical shipment was stuck in customs, and then . . .

Once upon a time, you dreamed a dream about being in business, and then . . .

"Once upon a time" isn't just for fairy tales. Because once upon a time really is a beginning.

That's the most important thing that all stories share, both the real ones and the made-up ones. Every story needs to start somewhere. It needs a beginning. The tricky thing with beginnings though, is they sometimes look like endings. The thing fails . . . the end. The idea falls flat . . . the end. There is no greater freedom then recognizing a beginning disguised as an end.

I realize that storytelling can be daunting. Sometimes we don't have a single idea. At other times we have so many that the paradox of choice keeps us frozen in place. It's easy to be intimidated by the blank page or the full auditorium. There are days when even the best storytellers freeze. But the way forward is always the same. The way forward is simply to begin.

"Once upon a time" may seem like an odd place to end our journey. But I think it's fitting. After all, the end of this story, this book, is really the beginning for you.

Once upon a time, I read a book about storytelling in business, and then . . .

Appendix

The Four-Story Cheat Sheet

	Value Story	Founder Story	Purpose Story	Customer Story
Purpose	More effective sales and marketing	Increased confidence in investors, partners, and employees	Team, organization alignment	Sales and marketing, fostering excellence
Primary Audience	Prospect / Customer	Stakeholders	Employees, teams	Prospect / Customer
Who Should Tell It	Marketers and salespeople	Entrepreneurs	Leaders, executives, and managers	Customers and companies

Acknowledgments

I think I always knew I would write books someday . . . What I didn't know was how much time, energy, effort, and sacrifice it would require of a whole team of people to make a book possible.

And it starts with the youngest, my sweet kiddos. Arn and Aune, thank you for sharing your life with this book. Thank you for waiting so patiently when I needed just a few more minutes to wrap up a chapter. Thank you for brainstorming titles and mocking up covers. Thank you for celebrating so genuinely when the manuscript was finally done. Thank you for traveling the country with me to get the book off the ground, forgoing lunch and finding your own way to the bathroom when the line for preorders stretched on for hours. Thank you for telling your teachers and your classmates and random people in airport lounges that your mama wrote a book and they should go buy it. You are the best six-year-old and seven-year-old a mama, or author, could ask for.

Though it may seem strange to thank someone whose name you don't know, this book wouldn't have happened if it weren't for the people sitting in the audiences of the conferences where I have had the honor to present. Thank you for listening, thank you for asking questions and sharing your stories, thank you for challenging me to shape this storytelling-thing that I've always just known how to do into a message that can be used. Even when the lights were too bright to see your faces, I could feel your energy, and I don't know where I'd be without you.

To those who read the early version of book and offered your endorsements, thank you. Your words of encouragement meant the world to me at that very vulnerable time. I'll admit—I fell out of my chair a couple of times with excitement, but the bruises were worth it.

I'll never forget the first time I heard about Kathy Schneider, my agent. I was at an airport, in the gate area, on the phone with Kate White, former editor-in-chief of *Cosmopolitan* magazine. She was generously giving me some book publishing advice, for which I am so grateful, and mentioned a friend of hers who was launching a new career as an agent at an agency looking to build their business book repertoire. A few days later, I was on the phone with Kathy. A few weeks later, I met with her at her office. A few minutes after meeting her, I knew she was the one. Thank you for your hard work and your emotional support—this book publishing thing is not for the weak! We set some high goals, Kathy, and I'm pretty proud of what these two first-timers accomplished. So much gratitude to you, Chris Prestia, and Julianne Tinari, and the whole JRA team.

A big thanks to Dan Clements, who helped get the words out of my head and onto paper for the first time. There is nothing worse than staring at a blank page; you made sure my pages were full from the start. To Beth Wand and Kristina Brune, thank you so much for showing up at crunch time. When the deadline was fierce and the time was limited, you stepped in and stepped up, and I am so grateful.

I'll never forget the first time I talked to my editor, Jessica. Of course, she wasn't my editor yet; she was interviewing me to see if it was a good fit. The interview happened via conference call, and I was sweating. Literally and figuratively. Jessica wasn't afraid to ask the tough questions and pushed me to clarify what this book was about and who would want to read it. When the call was over, I sunk back in my chair, exhausted. And I knew that if Jessica said yes, this book would be great. She did. And it is. With Jessica came the whole HarperCollins Leadership team: Jeff, Amanda, Hiram, Sicily, and many others. Thank you for believing in me and this message and bringing it to the world.

To my internal team—Tiffany, for helping me tell my stories on a daily basis via Instagram. To Meg, for spreading the word on social (and for being there to help that first crazy day we offered preorders). And to Andrea, my right hand. Thank you for making sure the rest of my business kept running while I was in and out of author mode.

Thank you to my friends and family who supported me and cheered me on and listened to me talk shop, even when you didn't want to. I couldn't have done this without you.

Finally, to Michael. The book starts with you, and it ends with you. As it should. I love you.

Notes

Introduction

1. "History," Eight & Bob, accessed February 5, 2019, https://eightandbob
.com/us/history/.

Chapter 1: The Gaps in Business and the Bridges
That Close (and Don't Close) Them

1. "Building Powerful Brands / Brand Revitalisation: Extra Gum—Give
Extra, Get Extra," The Marketing Society, accessed March 18, 2019,
https://www.marketingsociety.com/sites/default/files/thelibrary/Give
%20extra_Redacted.pdf.

2. Magnus Pagendarm and Heike Schaumburg, "Why Are Users Banner-
Blind? The Impact of Navigation Style on the Perception of Web
Banners," *Journal of Digital Information* 2, no. 1 (2001), https://journals
.tdl.org/jodi/index.php/jodi/article/view/36/38.

3. "Online Consumers Fed Up with Irrelevant Content on Favorite
Websites, According to Janrain Study," Janrain, July 31, 2013, https://
www.janrain.com/company/newsroom/press-releases/online-consumers
-fed-irrelevant-content-favorite-websites-according.

4. Melanie C. Green and Timothy C. Brock, "The Role of Transportation
in the Persuasiveness of Public Narratives," *Journal of Personality and
Social Psychology* 79, no. 5 (2000): 701–21, http://dx.doi.org/10.1037
/0022-3514.79.5.701.

5. T. Van Laer et al., "The Extended Transportation-Imagery Model: A
Meta-Analysis of the Antecedents and Consequences of Consumers'

213

Narrative Transportation," *Journal of Consumer Research* 40, no. 5 (February 2014): 797–817, https://doi.org/10.1086/673383.

6. Jillian Berman, "There's Something About Breath Mints and Sharing," *The Wall Street Journal*, September 11, 2017, https://www.wsj.com/articles/theres-something-about-breath-mints-and-sharing-1505135794.

7. "Building Powerful Brands," The Marketing Society.

8. "Building Powerful Brands," The Marketing Society.

Chapter 2: Once Upon a Brain

1. Paul J. Zak, "Why We Cry at Movies," *Psychology Today*, February 3, 2009, https://www.psychologytoday.com/blog/the-moral-molecule/200902/why-we-cry-movies.

2. Paul J. Zak, "Why Inspiring Stories Make Us React: The Neuroscience of Narrative," *Cerebrum* (January–February 2015): 2, https://www.ncbi.nlm.nih.gov/pmc/articles/PMC4445577/.

3. Zak, "Why Inspiring Stories Make Us React."

4. Zak, "Why Inspiring Stories Make Us React."

5. See Ushma Patel, "Hasson Brings Real Life into the Lab to Examine Cognitive Processing," *Princeton University News*, December 5, 2011, https://www.princeton.edu/main/news/archive/S32/27/76E76/index.xml.

6. Zak, "Why Inspiring Stories Make Us React."

7. Zak, "Why Inspiring Stories Make Us React."

8. Zak, "Why Inspiring Stories Make Us React."

Chapter 3: What Makes a Story Great

1. Chris Chase, "Seattle's Super Bowl Win Made Gambling History," *USA Today*, February 4, 2014, http://ftw.usatoday.com/2014/02/seattle-seahawks-super-bowl-prop-bets-odds.

2. Suzanne Vranica, "Higher Prices Don't Keep Marketers Away from Ad Time for Super Bowl," *The Wall Street Journal*, January 3, 2012, https://www.wsj.com/articles/SB10001424052970203899504577130940265401370.

3. Sherwood Forest, "Budweiser Super Bowl XLVIII Commercial—'Puppy Love,'" YouTube video, 1:00, January 31, 2014, https://www.youtube.com/watch?v=Zsj9AiK76Z4.

4. See Jill Rosen, "Super Bowl Ads: Stories Beat Sex and Humor, Johns Hopkins Researcher Finds," Hub, Johns Hopkins University, January 31, 2014, http://hub.jhu.edu/2014/01/31/super-bowl-ads/.

5. Yuval Noah Harari, *Sapiens: A Brief History of Humankind* (New York: Harper, 2015), 31.

6. "Why Choose hydraSense®," hydraSense Nasal Care, accessed February 5, 2019, https://www.hydrasense.com/why/naturally-sourced-seawater/.

7. Alli McKee, "[Your Company] in 100 Words," Medium, November 1, 2017, https://medium.com/show-and-sell/your-company-in-100-words -e7558b0b1077.

8. Marketwired, "Tivo's Top 10 Commercials From 50 Years of the Biggest Game of the Year," Yahoo! Finance, January 11, 2016, https://finance .yahoo.com/news/tivos-top-10-commercials-50-110000503.html.

9. "Super Bowl 2014 Ads: Facts and Figures (Updated)," Marketing Charts, February 6, 2014, http://www.marketingcharts.com/traditional/super -bowl-2014-ads-facts-and-figures-39421/.

10. Keith A. Quesenberry, "William Shakespeare Holds the Key to a Great Super Bowl Ad," *Time*, February 1, 2016, http://time.com/4200086/best -super-bowl-ads/.

11. NPR, "Code Switch: An Advertising Revolution," Stitcher, September 5, 2017, https://www.stitcher.com/podcast/national-public-radio/code -switch/e/51357262?autoplay=true.

Chapter 4: The Value Story

1. Daniel Kahneman, *Thinking, Fast and Slow* (New York: Farrar, Straus and Giroux, 2011), 20.

2. Kahneman, 20.

3. Kahneman, 62.

4. Amy Wolf, "For a Winning Ad at the Super Bowl: Less Shock and More Sophisticated Storyline," Vanderbilt News, January 30, 2012, https:// news.vanderbilt.edu/2012/01/30/winning-super-bowl-ads-needs -sophistication/.

5. Philip Elmer-Dewitt, "Why 'Misunderstood' Won an Emmy for Apple," *Fortune*, August 18, 2014, http://fortune.com/2014/08/18/why -misunderstood-won-an-emmy-for-apple/.

6. Elmer-Dewitt, "Why 'Misunderstood' Won an Emmy for Apple."

Chapter 5: The Founder Story

1. Biz Carson, "How 3 Guys Turned Renting an Air Mattress in Their Apartment into a $25 Billion Company," *Business Insider*, February 23,

2016, https://www.businessinsider.com/how-airbnb-was-founded-a
-visual-history-2016-2.

2. Michael Carney, "Brian Chesky: I Live on Cap'n McCain's and Obama O's Got AirBnB Out of Debt," Pando, January 10, 2013, https://pando .com/2013/01/10/brian-chesky-i-lived-on-capn-mccains-and-obama-os -got-airbnb-out-of-debt/.

3. Carolyn Said, "Airbnb's Swank Digs Reflect Growth, But Controversy Grows," SF Gate, January 27, 2014, https://www.sfgate.com/bayarea /article/Airbnb-s-swank-digs-reflect-growth-but-5175734.php.

4. Max Chafkin, "Can Airbnb Unite the World?" Fast Company, January 12, 2016, https://www.fastcompany.com/3054873 /can-airbnb-unite-the-world.

5. Said, "Airbnb's Swank Digs Reflect Growth."

6. Nat Levy, "Live Blog: Andreessen Horowitz Partner Jeff Jordan at the GeekWire Summit 2016," GeekWire, October 4, 2016, http://www .geekwire.com/2016/live-blog-andreessen-horowitz-partner-jeff-jordan -geekwire-summit-2016/.

7. Avery Hartmans, "This Is the One Quality Every Startup Founder Needs," Business Insider, September 25, 2016, http://www.businessinsider .com/jeff-jordan-andreessen-horowitz-startup-founders-2016-9.

8. Airbnb, "Funding Rounds," Crunchbase, https://www.crunchbase.com /organization/airbnb/funding_rounds/funding_rounds_list#section -funding-rounds.

9. 2017 Kaufman Index of Startup Activity, Ewing Marion Kauffman Foundation, May 2017, http://www.kauffman.org/kauffman-index /reporting/~/media/c9831094536646528ab012dcbd1f83be.ashx.

10. QuickBooks, "Did You Know? Most Small Businesses Start With $10,000 or Less," Intuit QuickBooks, accessed March 18, 2019, https://quickbooks .intuit.com/r/trends-stats/know-small-businesses-start-10000-less/.

11. Greg McKeown, "If I Read One More Platitude-Filled Mission Statement, I'll Scream," Harvard Business Review, October 4, 2012, https://hbr.org/2012/10/if-i-read-one-more-platitude-filled-mission -statement.

12. See "Number of U.S. Financial Advisers Fell for Fifth Straight Year—Report," Reuters, February 11, 2015, https://www.reuters.com /article/wealth-cerulli-advisor-headcount/number-of-u-s-financial -advisers-fell-for-fifth-straight-year-report-idUSL1N0VL23920150211.

Notes

Chapter 6: The Purpose Story

1. Paul J. Zak, "Why Your Brain Loves Good Storytelling," *Harvard Business Review*, October 28, 2014, https://hbr.org/2014/10/why-your -brain-loves-good-storytelling.
2. Simon Caulkin, "Companies with a Purpose Beyond Profit Tend to Make More Money," *Financial Times*, January 24, 2016, https://www .ft.com/content/b22933e0-b618-11e5-b147-e5e5bba42e51.
3. Rachel Tesler et al., "Mirror, Mirror: Guided Storytelling and Team Reflexivity's Influence on Team Mental Models," *Small Group Research* 49, no. 3 (2018): 267–305, https://journals.sagepub.com/doi/abs/10.1177 /1046496417722025.
4. Tesler et al., "Mirror, Mirror."
5. Tesler et al., "Mirror, Mirror."
6. Quoted in David K. Williams, "The Best Leaders Are Vulnerable," *Forbes*, July 18, 2013, https://www.forbes.com/sites/davidkwilliams /2013/07/18/the-best-leaders-are-vulnerable/#442fcf5e3c1d.
7. Williams, "The Best Leaders Are Vulnerable."
8. Williams, "The Best Leaders Are Vulnerable."
9. Robyn Fivush, Marshall Duke, and Jennifer G. Bohanek, "'Do You Know . . .' The Power of Family History in Adolescent Identity and Well-Being," *Journal of Family Life*, February 23, 2010, available at https://ncph.org/wp-content/uploads/2013/12/The-power-of-family -history-in-adolescent-identity.pdf.

Chapter 7: The Customer Story

1. "Local Consumer Review Survey 2018," BrightLocal, accessed March 18, 2019, https://www.brightlocal.com/learn/local-consumer-review-survey/.
2. Aaron Smith and Monica Anderson, "Online Shopping and E-Commerce: Online Reviews," Pew Research Center, December 19, 2016, http://www.pewinternet.org/2016/12/19/online-reviews/.
3. "Women's Deodorant: Reviews," Native, accessed February 5, 2019, https://www.nativecos.com/products/travel-deo-pack-womens -winter2018#reviews.
4. "Women's Deodorant: Reviews," Native.
5. Fay Schopen, "Outrage over McDonald's Twee 'Child Grief' Advert Is Plain Ridiculous," *The Guardian*, May 17, 2017, https://www.theguardian.com /commentisfree/2017/may/17/mcdonalds-child-grief-advert-bereavement.

Chapter 10: Telling Your Story

1. Khadeeja Safdar, "Now for Sale: The Empty Space Inside Retailers' Packages," *The Wall Street Journal*, July 22, 2018, https://www.wsj.com /articles/now-for-sale-the-empty-space-inside-retailers-packages -1532264400?mod=searchresults&page=1&pos=1.

2. Adaptly, with Refinery29 and Facebook, *The Science of Advertising: A Research Study on Sequenced for Call to Action vs. Sustained Call to Action*, Adaptly, accessed March 18, 2019, https://s3.amazonaws.com/sales .adaptly.com/The+Science+of+Social+Media+Advertising.pdf.

Conclusion

1. John K. Donahue and Melanie C. Green, "A Good Story: Men's Storytelling Ability Affects Their Attractiveness and Perceived Status," *Personal Relationships*, March 9, 2016, https://onlinelibrary.wiley.com/doi /full/10.1111/pere.12120.

About the Author

K indra Hall is a keynote speaker and award-winning storyteller. She has been published at Entrepreneur.com and Inc.com, and as a contributing editor to *Success* magazine. She speaks for and works with brands of all sizes to help them harness the power of storytelling.

Offstage, she lives in New York City with her husband and young son and daughter. She's an avid Soul Cycle rider, prefers the window seat on airplanes, and always drinks her coffee cold.

CALL FOR STORIES

Do you have a story about how you used
storytelling in your business? We would love
to hear it. Please send us your stories:
Hello@stellercollective.com

———

STELLER COLLECTIVE

If you or your team would like to put the
storytelling strategies you learned in this book
to work, please join us at an upcoming Steller
Storytelling Workshop event. To learn more about
the workshops and trainings, please visit:
www.stellercollective.com

———

BOOK KINDRA

To book Kindra Hall to speak at an
upcoming event, please contact:
Info@kindrahall.com